ZOE

A mother's gripping story of her daughter's fight for life!

ASHLEE MORRIS

WORLD WIDE
PUBLISHING GROUP

7710-T Cherry Park Dr, Ste 224

Houston, TX 77095

www.WorldwidePublishingGroup.com

Published in the United States of America

ISBN-13: 978-0692954225 (Worldwide Publishing Group)

ISBN-10: 0692954228

DEDICATION

I dedicate this book to my devoted family. My loving husband Chris Morris, our beautiful daughter Zoe Lee, and genius of a son, Zachary, Dad (Eddie Smith), and Mom (Alice Smith). This book is dedicated to the amazing first-responders, Troy and his Kangaroo Team. Finally, this book is dedicated to our remarkable surgeon, Dr. Sandi Lam.

Chris, honey, I cannot imagine the life-shaking event of facing death with our baby and not having you by my side. You sacrificed your time and comfort to be with us every day in the hospital; you allowed me the grace to feel and come to you in my darkest hours, you stood strong spiritually and gave God the praise as you saw the miracle and lived by faith from day one. *You are my rock. I love you.*

Zach, I am so grateful for your selfless humility in the weeks we've been away. You've given your time and allowed me to be by your sister's side in her struggle to get well. You've not once complained or made circumstances about yourself; you've always honored us and given us the freedom to feel and deal with the day-to-day demands of an unexpected brain injury. I will always remember weeping in your arms the day the doctors told us that Zoe would require surgery; you were so brave. *You give me strength. I love you.*

Precious Zoe, you don't quite understand all you've been through yet, but you're a strong, courageous little lady. Through your fight for life, you've inspired thousands to explore their relationship with God and call out to Him in prayer. You've ignited a fire in me and many others worldwide. You have the sweetest spirit; you're always looking to provide a smile to those around you. We don't know how much we truly love someone until they are almost taken from us. I love you with all my heart and can't wait to see how God uses you for His Kingdom glory. *You are the sunshine of our lives.*

Dad, words will never express the gratitude I have for you. You have selflessly served our family day and night not only through this life emergency, but always. You inspired me to share Zoe's story. I pray the Lord will richly bless you as you have always been such a tremendous blessing to our family. *You are strong like an eagle Daddy. I love you.*

Mom, Wow! I never expected this—not in a million years. Thank you for your steadfast intercession on behalf of our baby. Many times, I was so exhausted, the prayers were simply not there. That was okay because you never stopped. *Your fervent prayers and challenge to keep our prayer partners on track were crucial to our healing and God's miracle.*

I dedicate this book to the Lord, for preserving the life of our Zoe Lee. Lord, I gave my life to You as a six-year-old. I trusted you then, and I trust You now. *Life is complete when You are the Lord of it. I love You.*

CONTENTS

ACKNOWLEDGMENTS

Chris and I have been amazed by the generous support of our family, friends, community, and even total strangers. Thank each of you very much! We never, in a million years, expected this; but through your support, the excellent staff at Texas Children's Hospital, and God's grace we've experienced a 21st-century miracle.

Thank you, Robert (my oldest brother) and Missy Smith (his wife), who were a true source of spiritual encouragement and prayer support. Robert, thank you for setting up our Facebook Group, which became a support community that enabled more than 6,000 people, from many nations, to track our journey, pray for Zoe and our family. Within days of your creating Zoe's site, we had prayer support from friends around the world. Your time and effort made this possible.

Thank you, Missy, for bringing Zoe's sweet cousins, River and Brooke to see and encourage Zoe. You fought for those visits, and they were so very important.

Thank you, Julia Sharaby (my older sister), owner of two *Fusion Taco* restaurants in Houston. Thank you for feeding our guests and us at the hospital numerous times; and, for going out of your way to deliver personal hygiene items, clothes, and more. I love you.

Thank you, Bryan and Alexa Smith (my older brother and his wife) for bringing us delicious home-cooked meals, allowing us access to your home nearby as a place to get away, do laundry, shower, and for scheduling hair appointments for me. My priorities! Bryan, thank you for Zoe's gift. She loves her lemon purse and loves *you*. You developed her speech in the first few days after surgery. "Life gives us lemons at times. But, we'll always choose to make the best of it. Make lemonade!" Thanks for bringing Zoe's cousin, Karmin, for visits, and allowing her to have a one-of-a-kind Texas Children's Hospital slumber party!

Thank you, Mom, (Alice Smith, Zoe's "Meme"), and your friends; and Chris' mother, (Nancy Nolan, Zoe's "Nani"), who prayed and encouraged others to pray. I am grateful to you two for fighting for Zoe's healing and restoration.

Zoe and Chris' mother, Nancy; and her mother,
Yolanda Ojeda.

Thank you, Mathew and Danielle (Chris' brother and sister), and Alejandro, for the visits, gifts and encouraging video calls to Zoe. You brought smiles to our family during a helpless time.

Dad, thank you for being strong for me in my weakest hours. You slept countless nights in the cold ICU, forfeiting your comfort so we could rest. You inspired me, and I love you with all my heart.

To my beautiful, strong sisters of both mom's prayer team and my group of personal friends, I love you. Your visits, texts, help at my home, trips to therapy, meals and more brought me such joy and encouragement. To the friends, neighbors and family who called, prayed, visited and brought encouragement, we love you and feel so blessed to have you in our lives. Chrissy, Jean, Angie, and Rebecca, your constant loving support challenges me to be my best. I love you.

Thank you, Grammy nominee and multiple Dove Award winning contemporary Christian singer and songwriter, Kari Jobe. Your Skyped-in visit meant SO much to Zoe and our family. Zoe has memorized many of your songs, and we love hearing her accompany you. I drew strength from your God-ordained songs in my most desperate hours. I'll forever remember hearing you worship as we fought through the unknown. [Note: Watch Kari's visit with Zoe via Skype in Chapter 10.]

Thank you, NFL legend and defensive end for the Houston Texans, J.J. Watt, for your thoughtful personal video encouragement for Zoe. She is one of your smallest, yet biggest, fans. P.S. We watched this so many times, God's love shows through you!

Thank you, gospel and contemporary Christian recording artist, American Idol's Mandisa. Your Facebook Post of blessing to our daughter and concern for her recovery was such a surprise and encouragement. She loves to sing along with your recordings.

Chris and I choose to live our lives with gratitude. My life changed the day I chose to focus my attention on being grateful. I know we've missed the mention of gifts, calls, and cards received. Each of them was a blessing. Thank you for your support. We treasure you, and your part of this challenging journey our family has faced. <3

I freely quote in this book from some of our friends' Facebook posts. It was impossible for me to obtain permission. If you find your post quoted, or not quoted, thank you for understanding.

FOREWORD

Courage, generosity, and the miraculous.

I've rarely seen more faith in God, courage, and divine determination than Chris and Ashlee have shown when faced with such an emotionally-crushing event as they have, with their darling Zoe, several weeks ago.

I've rarely seen more generosity as their Facebook friends, and members of our family have shown with their prayers, words of encouragement, and gifts in support of Zoe's recovery. She has a long road ahead of her, but their friendship has provided much-needed comfort.

I've rarely seen such a miraculous act of God. The surgeons were quite clear about all that could go wrong. Ashlee, Zoe's mother, recently ran into the anesthesiologist who rolled Zoe into the surgical suite for emergency life-saving surgery. When he saw Zoe, he was shocked to see her so healthy. He admitted that as they prepared for surgery, there was a doubt that she would even survive. After five weeks in the hospital, three of them in a medically-induced coma, to see her enjoying the rest of her summer, even with several areas of therapy, is a miracle.

We thank our loving heavenly Father; remarkable neurosurgeon, Dr. Sandi K. Lam; and the wonderful staff at Texas Children's Hospital (Main Campus) in Houston, Texas.

More: http://tinyurl.com/Zoes-Surgeon

--Eddie Smith, Zoe's Pawpaw

INTRODUCTION

In the early days of bone weary Intensive Care, at any time, we had 20 to 30 people clustered at the hospital to visit Zoe and offer us support. The love, prayers, gifts of food, and people coming to worship and hold all night prayer services in the chapel blessed us. We will never forget the support we received. Thank you.

Several people had asked what I needed, many of my dear friends brought us thoughtful care packages. Frankly, my biggest need was for a curling iron and hair straightener! Judy Graham, and my sister, Julia Sharaby, put together a bag of nice shampoos, conditioners and a body soap that I loved. It's interesting how God uses the simple things in our lives to speak to us, as you will read below.

We didn't have beds or a private place to sleep. Instead, we had a small corner of a room filled with dozens of leather recliners that parents with heavy hearts slept on next to us. I remember the first night we walked into this room being shocked to see how many parents were sleeping in the ICU.

I would wash my face every night in the public bathroom, then walk through the halls of the hospital back to my recliner in my pajamas. You who know me well can verify this alone is my biggest nightmare!

Some nights we were chosen for a complimentary stay at the *Ronald McDonald House*. It was a treat to have a soft bed and a shower. God bless the people who serve this ministry.

During most of those private showers, I was crying out to God to save my baby's life, while trying to savor a little peace.

It was on one of those mornings, as I showered in the hospital, that I used the last drop of my amazing soap. Suddenly, I felt God telling me this part of our journey was over, finished. Seems silly, right? But that's the way God often speaks to me. It's typically in everyday situations with small things. It doesn't take a revival or a mission trip to some other country for me to feel God's presence; although being in Nigeria, Uganda, and other developing nations has taught me to be grateful, and how to love people. I've enjoyed my personal relationship with the Holy Spirit, who gently speaks to me wherever I am.

When our Facebook Group was established, it was quickly filled with several thousand members from many different backgrounds. I received a message from one guy who said that he didn't believe in God, but he was praying for Zoe, because (his words) "what could it hurt?"

I'm amazed that we came from such different places, with one heart and focus—on the survival of a five-year-old girl. I'm a Christian who believes in the Holy Spirit. I don't have to be in church to feel God's presence because the Lord is with me, living inside of me all the time. I know that's not what everyone believes or has experienced. I treasure every prayer that was prayed for Zoe.

Thank you for helping us bear our burden. Mere words will never express my gratitude.

1

SLEEP INTERRUPTED!

My husband, Chris and I had only been asleep a couple of hours when at 11:30 PM, Monday night, May 22nd, 2017 the blood-curdling screams of our beautiful five-year-old daughter, Zoe, abruptly woke us up. That made no sense at all. If she'd had a bad dream, Zoe would have come to our room and jumped into bed with us. *This time was much different.* Her screams of, "Mommy! Mommy! Mommy!" were growing louder and louder. Something was desperately wrong.

We bolted from our bed, ran through the house and found her in our kitchen, wandering around with no sense of direction, a blank stare on her face, spitting from her mouth.

Chris loudly asked, "Zoe, Zoe, what's wrong!?" She continued to scream. She seemed not to hear us, or make eye contact with us. I assumed she'd had a bad dream, and was sleep walking.

Frantically, as Chris tried to wake her to determine what happened, I went to check on her older brother, Zachary. His lights were out, and he was in his bed. I asked if everything was okay. He said that he too was startled by Zoe's screams, but assumed she was okay when the screams died down.

Confused and concerned, as Chris continued to tend to Zoe, I checked her room and found her bed covered with vomit. My maternal instincts kicked in. I pulled her soiled bedding off and started a load of laundry.

When I returned to the kitchen, Chris had no further clues as to what had caused Zoe to wake in such panic. However, she did seem to be quieting down. She still made no eye contact with us. Clueless, we assumed her upset stomach would soon pass. So, we made a comfortable spot for her on the floor near our bed and had her lay down. That way, she'd be close to us if she needed anything further.

We grew further alarmed when we laid Zoe down, and she began to gag. Her eyes rolled to the back of her head, and she moaned and groaned in sheer agony. Panic gripped us both. What could this be? We felt helpless and confused as we drew a warm bath, placed her in it, and gently splashed water on her. Still, there were no words or eye contact. Chris lifted Zoe gently under her arms from the tub and stood her on her feet so we could dry her. But both of Zoe's legs gave way, and she collapsed in our arms unconscious.

Chris shouted at me, "Get what you need, it's time to go!"

In eleven years of marriage, I'd never heard such despair in my husband's voice. I ran back to Zach's room and told him that Zoe was sick, and we needed to take her to the emergency room. Zachary, fourteen-years-old at the time, had important high school exams the following day. Thinking we would be back shortly, I encouraged him to try to get some rest.

I grabbed my sweater, Zoe's blanket, and her "Lamby," her beloved stuffed animal. When I got to Chris' truck Zoe was unconscious, in her car seat, propped up by the door, her eyes closed, and completely unresponsive.

How could this be happening? Not even two hours earlier she was giggling, laughing, and happily running around the house, throwing a tennis ball for her dog, Sophie! The day before, Zoe had been joyously dancing at church to her favorite praise song, "Good, Good Father;" and eating pink sprinkle-covered donuts with a bright, healthy smile on her face.

Although I felt the normal motherly panic, I optimistically assumed this was a stomach bug. After all, she had vomited in her bed. She would surely be alright with the right medication... Or would she?

2

NEIGHBORHOOD 24/7 EMERGENCY ROOM

Chris rushed down the street, around the corner and swerved into the neighborhood 24-hour Emergency Room parking lot, slammed on the brakes, and skidded to a stop. He jumped out with the motor left running. He grabbed his baby Zoe into his arms and ran as fast as he could through their front door.

I don't recall the words exchanged, but when the people at the front desk saw the concern on Chris' face, within seconds, we were in a trauma room filled with medical personnel. The doctor on-call heard our concern for her stomach, but seemed to ignore us completely. Instead, he frantically yelled at the team for a CT scan of Zoe's brain. I remember feeling like he had lost his mind, why in the world would he scan her brain? I thought, *for goodness sake, she threw up in her bed. This is clearly a stomach issue.*

The team swirled around us, and in minutes she was on the table, and we were behind a glass window watching the machine scan her abdomen and brain. We held our breath and watched as the scan results slowly appeared on the machine's monitor. The scan from the base of her skull to the top of her head looked black and grayish. To our untrained eyes, all looked normal until we both saw a golf ball-sized white area appear on the left side.

We were suddenly gripped by fear. What was it? Surely it wasn't normal. Then the technician explained cautiously that this wasn't her specialty, so she couldn't share any results with us. Well, it didn't take a professional for us to understand there was *much more* to the picture than we'd realized.

All the attending physician told us was that there was blood present in Zoe's brain and that he had called for a Life Flight emergency helicopter, which was on its way to transport her to Texas Children's Hospital (Main Campus). We were in total shock as they questioned us about any possibility of physical abuse, an accidental fall, her having been pushed down on the playground, or if she and Zachary had been wrestling.

I knew that Zoe hadn't fallen that day. In fact, when she came home from school she was grinning from ear to ear because teachers, Mrs. Bremer and "Mrs. Coach Tucker," had allowed her to pick a special treat from the school treasure box. Had she been pushed or fallen, she would have shared that with me as well. After all, we're not only mother and daughter; we are best friends.

I excused myself, stepped outside, and calmly called Zach to wake him and ask if he had witnessed anything that could have caused this injury. As I slipped away, I noticed that a Harris County Sheriff's Deputy followed me to eavesdrop on our conversation. It was clear that they were watching me. I'm now in a life or death situation, and *under investigation?*

I explained to Zach that the scan showed there was a bit of blood on sister's brain, and asked if they had wrestled earlier that day. That wouldn't have been uncommon. He's taught his sissy to be tough. Uncharacteristically, Zach burst into tears and said that nothing, absolutely nothing, had happened that could've hurt her. I knew the pressure the police and staff had put on me. My stomach churned to feel that I was interrogating my son. But we were helplessly searching for answers to what might have caused our Zoe to be in such danger.

It was well after midnight when we were advised that Life Flight was on its way and that we would be flown downtown to Texas Children's Hospital. I argued that there was a branch of the hospital down the street and that I'd prefer to be taken there, immediately. The doctor looked at me with tears in his eyes and said, "Ma'am, if this child were my daughter, I'd fight for her to be taken to their main campus. It is truly the best of the best, and your Zoe is in *very serious condition.*"

Seeing a doctor in tears made my heart skip a beat. I tried hard to stay calm for Zoe. Up until this point, I was singing her favorite worship songs, and tickling her arms, while she lay in front of me unresponsive. When I saw the concern on his face, I looked around and realized that everyone there felt the same. *We were in a life or death struggle for my baby.*

After what seemed like an eternity, I overheard the staff fretfully discussing issues concerning our transportation. I heard the Life Flight chopper circling overhead, but we were in a neighborhood emergency facility. There was no helipad here. There wasn't even a reasonably safe place to land. Plus, a heavy fog was setting in. We had wasted what felt like an eternity for that helicopter, and now it was impossible for it to land. We were devastated. Looking back now, I know *this was all part of God's plan!* Had Zoe flown at a higher altitude, with those sensitive vessels leaking blood into her brain, she may have experienced more brain damage—even death.

Suddenly a crew of ambulance first responders exploded into the room and began frantically hooking Zoe to all sorts of machines. The ER Doctor demanded intubation. With that order, they sedated Zoe and put an adolescent/adult size tube down her throat to begin breathing for her.

Seeing that, I screamed at the Lord from the foot of her bed, "God, now is the time! I *know* you're a God of miracles! I need you to come from heaven to earth and touch my baby, Father. *We need YOU!*" I begged and pleaded with God to touch our Zoe as I watched them prepare her for the trip. Chris and I held onto each other for support. My giant of a husband collapsed in tears too.

My mother, Alice Smith is a well-known author, teacher and prayer leader. She had just returned from a two-week ministry trip to South Korea and Japan, hours before we found ourselves in this nightmare. I had tried desperately to get a hold of her, or my dad, for 30 minutes, but they were not answering their phones. Finally, I called our close family friend, Nick, and asked him to drive over, ring their doorbell, and wake them.

A few minutes later my phone rang with a concerned call from my parents. Chris asked Troy, the leader of *Texas Children's Kangaroo Crew*, a mobile intensive care ambulance for children, for more information. Chris begged for an update of any kind. "Can you at least tell us if she's stable?" Troy looked down, then hesitantly replied, "No, sir. She's not stable." I knew by the look on his face that he didn't expect Zoe to live.

Grief has never felt more real, we were losing our child, and we had no control over the outcome. On the phone, I told my mother that Zoe was gravely ill, and she and Dad needed to meet us at the hospital. Since I didn't know how much longer we might have Zoe, I asked if she and Dad would pick up Zachary at our house and bring him with them to Texas Children's Hospital, downtown. I continued my warfare praying until they put Zoe in the ambulance.

By then, Chris' mother, Nancy Nolan, had joined us. She and Chris followed the ambulance in Chris' truck, while I rode with Zoe in the ambulance. Rushing down Interstate 10 (Katy Freeway) toward downtown Houston, with lights flashing and sirens screaming, I asked the driver of our *Kangaroo Crew* if he was a believer, he graciously said he was. He said that he knows God performs miracles, because of his mother, who was given less than a year to live, is alive and well years later, and is a worship leader today.

I loved his story, but try as I might, I couldn't shake the sadness I felt. We prayed the entire way to the hospital. The siren sounds inexplicably stopped. Chris, who was following close behind, called in a panic. Rumor is, when the lights are on without a siren, the patient has expired, and the emergency is over. His heart was gripped with fear, thinking we had lost Zoe.

I looked over my shoulder at her on the gurney, and the crew assured me that her heart was still beating. Minutes later, we entered Houston's famed Medical Center, and approached the emergency room entrance at Texas Children's Hospital.

3

WHAT WAS HAPPENING TO OUR BABY?

While we had a perfect little family of three, I'd always wanted a sibling for Zach. In December 2010, Chris and I made the brave decision to try for our family expansion. Baby Zoe was conceived within a month! We were delighted to be pregnant, and to receive whatever God gave us. But, I secretly hoped for a little girl.

We should have known she was a fighter from the start. She always kicked Daddy's hands from my belly, did flips and gymnastics. I loved my pregnancy, but she was an active little lady.

A few years prior, my mom, Alice Smith, "Meme," had given me a tiny simple pink onesie and shared with me that God told her we'd have a baby girl, and she would be unique to the Lord. At that time, I kindly accepted the gift but laughed. We were only discussing the "what ifs," and not ready to make the jump.

The day the doctor told us we were expecting Zoe, our baby girl, I knew this was God's child. He'd shown her to us in the spirit realm, and she was our gift from Him. Pregnancy was fun and easy. My mother-in-law, Nancy Nolan, "Nani," cooks Cuban food. So, during my pregnancy, we usually enjoyed Sunday lunch at her house, with my feet up. Every checkup was wonderful and encouraging. Zach's was a cesarean birth, so Zoe was arriving with scheduled delivery. It would be an easy breezy cover girl, right? Quite literally, I had highlighted my hair, put on my makeup, and Meme ordered a fashionable hospital gown for me. They gave me meds that made me itch, but within hours, we had a gorgeous, 7lb 15oz healthy baby girl.

We named her, Zoe Lee Morris. "Zoe" is the biblical Greek word for life. "Lee" is my mother's middle name, and part of the spelling of my first name. Then, of course, her proud daddy's last name, Morris. After all, she is a "daddy's girl."

She was an outgoing, thoughtful, friendly, vivacious little thing. Princess-loving, worship-singing, jazz-dancing, rock star. Healthy as a horse. We never dealt with a broken bone, a sprained ankle, or serious illness of any kind. She was in gymnastics, making good grades in school, jumping on our backyard trampoline, and playing hard all day, every day. Zoe was a busy girl. But she was never too busy for the needs of others. She loved to pray and care for the needs of those around her.

So…

How…

Could this be happening?

4

ARRIVAL AT TEXAS CHILDREN'S HOSPITAL ER

It was 2:30 AM when the ambulance crew quickly wheeled Zoe into the massive hospital's triage room. Immediately 12-15 professionals of varying ages, ethnicities, and specialties raced to her bedside. Our families arrived shortly after, as did a hospital chaplain, a young lady, who politely offered to pray with us. "Of course," we said, "we welcome all prayer."

Just like in the movies, they loudly shouted the details of her condition: "Five-year-old female, suffered an undiagnosed brain-bleed, left lobe of the brain..." Our family doctor, Dr. Greg Walker, and his wife Debbie (an experienced RN) who had been called walked in and asked for the chain of events. We explained all that had happened. I still associated Zoe having vomited in her sleep with stomach issues, and was worried that I had over-fed her late in the evening. I had worked late that night and brought home sandwiches around 9:00 PM.

Had my feeding her so late caused her stomach to be upset as she slept, then to vomit and burst a blood vessel in her brain? I had quickly made her situation my fault, and the world was lying heavily on my shoulders until Dr. Walker explained that there was no way my theory could be true. I cried with relief, but that didn't change the fact that our beautiful Zoe was dying before our eyes. The Walkers spent the entire night with us, explaining in layman's terms what the medical team was telling us. They allayed so many of our fears. We had the best medical team in the world, yet still felt so afraid.

After an hour of testing, Zoe was rushed to another CT scan, then taken to the Intensive Care Unit on the third floor. We gathered there with our closest friends and family, then for the next 24 hours we took shifts, watching our daughter, who had tubes in her nose, her mouth, and several IVs that pumped meds into her seemingly lifeless body while a machine pumped air into her lungs, taking each breath for her.

I can't even put into words how shocking it was to see this transformation within hours of our arrival.

We filled Zoe's Intensive Care room with beautiful pictures of her in better days. Her Nani brought several framed photos so the medical staff would understand who we were fighting for.

Hopelessness tried desperately to gain a grip on our hearts. We *would not* allow it. We told ourselves, "Our God is good. He is greater than what we see this morning."

The doctors felt like we would see the bleeding stopped, and that the brain would naturally heal itself. Us? We had no idea what to expect. Seeing her in this condition was devastating.

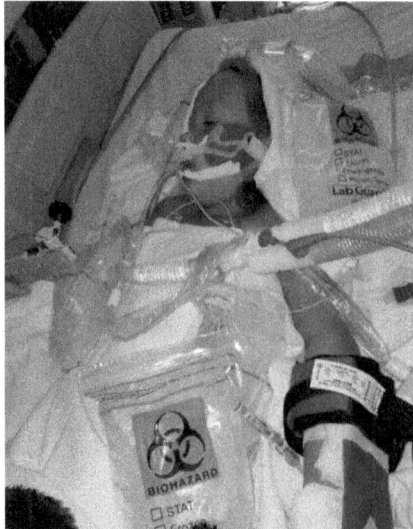

ZOE

One of our close family friends, Wyona Freysteinson (Zoe's "Amma"), is an Associate Professor in the College of Nursing at Texas Women's University. She arrived at the ICU waiting room, like many others. She was quite familiar with what Zoe was experiencing and spent many hours the first two days explaining the crisis we faced. She helped us understand each assessment and option the physicians gave us. It was certainly reassuring to have her by our side. Amma loves Zoe dearly and has "adopted her" as one of her own grandchildren.

Within hours, the doctors ordered a repeat CT Scan (Computerized tomography scan using X-ray), plus an MRI (Magnetic Resonance Imaging scan that produces greater detail). They also called for an Angiogram (X-ray scan using a dye to photograph blood flow in a vessel or vein), which meant that they would pump dye into Zoe's bloodstream to "light up" any broken vessels which may have been the source of the bleeding.

As the somber medical techs wheeled Zoe's tiny body down the white, chilled hallways for those tests, Chris and I followed. We prayed and pled the blood of Jesus over her as we loudly played Kari Jobe's song, *You Are for Me*; and Hillsong's, *It is Well With My Soul* on my cell phone. Rather than be influenced by what we saw, we thanked God in advance for what we could not yet see. We proclaimed that His miracle would be done in, and through her life.

A grandmotherly woman named Kathy greeted us in the MRI, CT Scan and Angiogram testing area. She hugged me, and assured us that she'd be with Zoe and would look after her as if she was one of her own. God bless those nurses and assistants who go above and beyond their duties to make a personal, positive connection with distraught families. Kathy's thirty seconds of reassurance and her kind hug were so meaningful to me in my time of desperation. Thank you, Kathy!

Chris and I signed page after page of medical forms detailing the worst-case scenarios of possible complications that could arise from blood transfusions and general anesthesia. We were certain that God was in control of our baby. However, we had no understanding of what we were facing. We kissed Zoe Lee goodbye, praying that it would only be a temporary separation.

The temperature in the waiting room was cold, and the lights were bright. However, at that point, we hadn't slept for over 24 hours. Chris and I shared Zoe's large stuffed animals as pillows. I put Chris' hat over my head, he wore his sunglasses, and we fell into a deep sleep trusting our heavenly Father and the doctors with our five-year-old daughter.

An hour later we woke up from what felt like a full night's sleep and saw Robert, my oldest brother, sitting across from us. We laughed as we told him how creepy it was that he was watching us sleep. He smiled and said he'd been praying for our peace the entire time. He held me as we wept and prayed.

Finally, the medical team emerged with Zoe's MRI results. The MRI revealed that the bleeding had stopped, *praise God!* Her brain was no longer continuing to bleed. The bad news was that it was due to the pressure build-up from swelling in the brain. It was as if you were to apply pressure to an open wound on your arm or leg to stop the bleeding. The swelling in Zoe's brain was the pressure that had stopped the bleeding.

However, the swelling could permanently damage her brain. And what would happen if the pressure and swelling went down? Would the bleeding continue? Was this good news, or was it scarier long-term? Our emotions were raw, as additional results poured in.

Next came the Angiogram report, which revealed that Zoe had a rare brain malformation called an AVM, an acronym for Arteriovenous Malformation, which is a rare congenital disability, that less than 1% of the population has. The doctor explained that an AVM is a cluster of tiny blood vessels that connect with an artery, which commonly results in an aneurysm or brain-bleed. Some people with AVMs live their entire lives without a problem. When adults with AVMs do experience a brain-bleed, they rarely survive. Because we had caught this at Zoe's young age meant that they would likely be able to save her life.

The neurologist explained that in Zoe's case a blood vessel deep in the left side of her brain had burst; and was so deep that surgery was not an option. Surgery could do more damage than good. The doctors would attempt to treat it medically and hope for natural healing. We could only pray that the bleeding would stop, the pressure would subside, and the blood that had accumulated in her head would dry and clear away over time.

The doctors speculated that the best treatment for Zoe might be to destroy the AVM with radiation. They would, however, need to wait a year or more for Zoe's brain to heal before they could do this treatment. We were grasping for any kind of hope. Honestly, to have Zoe this close to death; then for her to live for another year or two with the threat of another deadly brain bleed (an aneurysm) was of little comfort.

We had high faith in the Lord, yet such uncertainty. Was Zoe already brain dead? Was it the machines that kept her breathing on her own, or had her body shut down when she collapsed in our home?

Chris and I took turns being "the strong one." Without fail or any planning, he cried and wept, while I was strong — then, vice versa. We needed each other more than ever before.

Robert stayed with us while the doctors delivered their reports. He felt encouraged and offered to share the news with the twenty or so family and friends who anxiously awaited upstairs. This was such a relief. One moment, I was hopeful and confident; the next, I was tired, confused, hopeless, desperate, and afraid.

Can I be real with you? As he left, I looked at Chris and admitted that I didn't feel any better. I couldn't explain it. As a Christian, I believe in the power of God's healing touch. I believe the blood of Jesus is more than enough. I knew God heard my prayers and He was with me. But, I didn't feel we had gained much encouragement from the scans. New information, yes; but no improvement to speak of, or impact on our darling daughter's behalf.

It's easier to *say* the Word than to *stand on it* in your darkest hour. The Apostle Paul says in 2 Corinthians 4:18 AMP, "*So we look not at the things which are seen, but at the things which are unseen; for the things which are visible are temporal* [just brief and fleeting], *but the things which are invisible are everlasting and imperishable.*" I was confused by how some considered the fact that the bleeding had stopped was good news. Yes, but we had much more to consider. Would Zoe live a normal life? Would she even come home from this? There were no guarantees, just empty thoughts, empty, dangerous thoughts.

Chris and I took turns resting on the leather recliners *outside* her ICU room. The staff encouraged us to maintain "low/no stimulation." They explained that although she was unconscious, she could likely hear everything around her. If she recognized our voices, it could provoke unwanted brain stimulation. How strange it was to visit our precious baby from behind glass doors. She had been in a medically-induced coma for two days, with no further plans for her treatment.

The next day my sister, Julia came to visit with a teddy bear for Zoe, and food for our family and guests. It reminded me of Jesus' feeding of the 5,000 in the Bible. The delicious food she brought from her amazing restaurant, *Fusion Taco*, warmed our hearts and filled our stomachs. It kept us full, and remarkably, it seemed to multiply every time we went into snack room.

As I wrestled with sadness and despair, some of our family took the opportunity to minister to several other hurting families whose children were in the ICU. Zoe's story was already influencing lives. As one family was saying their goodbyes to their son, I came to terms with the realization that not every child would make it out of children's ICU alive.

That afternoon Zoe's temperature suddenly spiked. An electric blanket was monitoring it. Her body temperature slowly crept up from 98.6 to 99 degrees, and within five minutes it reached to more than 104 degrees. Where was the staff? Why were they unresponsive? Alarmed, I frantically screamed at the nurses nearby demanding Tylenol. I felt that I could've jogged to the pharmacy for Tylenol faster than they were responding. After all, we were in one of the most prestigious children's hospitals in the world, right?

Within seconds of thinking that, a team swarmed into the room, and in a flash, they gave Zoe some meds and covered her from head to toe with plastic bags filled with ice. A few hours later, the neurologists came in. They explained that an ICP monitor (an Intracranial Pressure Monitor) needed to be screwed into Zoe's skull to measure the amount of pressure on her brain. We could hardly breathe! What? They were now going to drill a hole in the top of our baby's head and screw in a pressure gauge!? Had we gone from healing naturally, to this? Chris and I sat there stunned and numb.

As any parent would, Chris and I challenged the idea. We calmly explained that tests had been run, which showed that her brain was healing on its own. An ICU nurse tried her best to explain to us that we needed to be open and patient. She said that each day would bring new information, which would lead to new treatment options. We weighed our options, then reluctantly signed the release for them to implant the pressure gauge, trusting the team knew what was best for our daughter. We prayed that we had made the right decision.

ICU was so hard. Due to the broad nature of all that had happened to Zoe's little body so quickly, they assigned several teams of specialists to her care. One doctor would give us hope; then a moment later, another would seem to contradict what we had just been told. Lots of people encouraged us to talk to our baby and comfort her; but the doctors were telling us overstimulation could cause harm. There were so many contradictions, nothing seemed settled.

These amazing doctors work many hours and under very trying conditions. They also must deal with their own emotions and concern for the children and families they serve. Zoe's constantly changing condition often left us confused and unsettled.

I am a strong, not easily shaken woman. But I felt so weak and helpless at times. I was exhausted and had tons of unanswered questions. I wouldn't say I was exactly fearful, but I was certainly uncertain at times. Our friends were broadcasting our situation to prayer chains, prayer groups, and praying people via social media. People all over the world were beginning to carry our burden in prayer. We could feel the impact of their prayers for Zoe! Chris and I discussed the unnatural peace that we felt at times. Go, God!

For the next 24-hours we were fixated on Zoe's ICP monitor. Strangely, it would show extreme brain pressures, then drop dramatically, though nothing was happening around her to stimulate those results.

Wednesday afternoon we were visiting with friends when the doctors asked to see us. It was nerve-racking. Every moment of those first few days was critical. Zoe was stable one moment, then in a life-threatening condition the next. I felt myself becoming calloused. Perhaps for self-preservation, I didn't allow my hopes to rise too high, but I wasn't accepting fear either. It was the only way I could cope. I suppose every parent in such circumstances develops their way of processing the trauma.

One of the requirements for any of us to enter Zoe's room was that we thoroughly wash our hands. The next time we walked in, a dozen doctors were swarming the hallway near her room. This visit didn't feel like the rest. Our familiar doctor started to speak, but was interrupted by a neurosurgeon, Dr. Sandi Lam. Dr. Lam firmly explained to the others that since this was her specialty, she preferred to be the one to explain things.

Turning her attention to us, she said that the pressure in Zoe's brain was not lessening as they had hoped and that the longer the brain experienced those high-pressure spikes, the more likely we'd see long-term brain damage. The bottom line was: Zoe required emergency brain surgery, which would begin immediately and last eight hours.

Dr. Lam explained that using the scans they had taken, the surgeons would spend three to four hours "mapping" Zoe's brain to determine the best approach to reach and remove the AVM deep inside, which was the source of the bleeding.

My heart sank, I was devastated. The surgeon said that Zoe had lost quite a bit of blood from the brain-bleed, which would require an immediate blood transfusion. The option to remove the AVM next year was *out!* They would remove it *now*. Zoe's life depended on it!

Dr. Lam said she felt optimistic that Zoe would make it through surgery alive, but she would likely have extreme weakness, or like some stroke victims, possibly lose the entire function of her right side. She explained that the blood was pooling on the thought processing and speech areas of Zoe's brain. Even if they could successfully remove the AVM, we would most likely see those areas affected.

Zoe might survive, but be unable to speak? Without surgery, death, and if not death, very little quality of life. We tearfully signed the papers, and released an emergency message to our family! Soon, dozens of friends and all our local family members flooded the waiting room.

5

EMERGENCY BRAIN SURGERY

When Zoe's brother Zach, who is taller than me, walked in, I was so overwhelmed with sadness that I fell into his arms and wailed uncontrollably. What was happening to us? Our children had always been healthy, never sick, rarely had either of them ever missed a day of school. Of course, I'd heard stories of families with serious illnesses. I'd seen disabled children in church, or at the grocery store. I often thought God hadn't given me children with such challenges because He knew I wasn't patient enough to handle it.

As if he was an adult, my 14-year-old Zach held me while I poured out my heart and transparently shared those thoughts with him. I asked if this was God's way of strengthening me, or perhaps a test to show me that I was strong enough to parent a disabled child. My questions were senseless really, but the strength I felt in my son's arms, made sense. We didn't understand how we got there, but we held each other with the strength and knowledge that we would face whatever came and trusted God for His best.

The medical team moved around us, continuing with their jobs, which included tons of graphic paperwork, which explained how everything during Zoe's surgery could turn for the worse in the blink of an eye. The team rehearsed the risks associated with blood transfusions, but explained that she might not make it through surgery without one. They needed to add someone else's blood to Zoe's to even start the surgery. We prayed that the donated blood was safe.

We must have signed six forms with three different people talking about the transfusions and risks. I was frustrated. Chris was in shock. Why were we wasting all this time talking about blood loss and transfusions when we were facing a life and death emergency? My close, dear friend, Rebecca spoke over me loudly to the team, "We accept any, and all transfusions." She said, "We are family. Zoe is my other daughter, and we accept." The attendant quickly pointed to all the places we'd need to sign and initial. We completed the forms, and they left.

Once things settled a bit, Rebecca explained to me the religious restrictions regarding blood transfusions. The staff was diligent to get their point across, and I respect that. I hugged Rebecca and wept. I felt so grateful for her presence at that moment.

When things calmed, I went to gather the nurses who had been with me the previous day when Zoe's temp was rising. I cried and repented for having screamed at them. I asked them to forgive me and thanked each of them for serving us. I emphasized that I trusted them.

One nurse cried with me. Another thanked me for coming back to do this and with a hug, admitted that she would probably have had the same reaction if it were her baby. God was working in my heart, imparting grace to others. The clock was ticking. Each of our family members came to say their goodbyes. We'd soon leave for surgery.

Again, just like three days earlier, we were wheeling our precious princess through the chilly, white, sterile hospital halls. Along the way, I played one of Zoe's favorite worship songs on my cell phone, Hilary Scott's, "Thy Will Be Done." Zoe is the most spiritual five-year-old I've ever known, although I'm likely a bit biased. :) Hilary had written her song during a sad time of despair after she had experienced a miscarriage.

Zoe *always* loved to sing along with this song, so I felt it was important that she understand its meaning. I had told her that Hilary had lost her baby. Her baby went to heaven instead of being born to her mommy. Hilary wrote the song to tell Jesus that she trusted His plan for her even during the time of such sadness and loss.

As the song played and we drew closer to the surgical suite, once again we gave Zoe Lee Morris to our heavenly Father. "Thy will be done, Lord." God's presence was with us every step of the way. Chris and I knew realistically that it might be the last time we would see our baby girl alive, but even with that, God's peace surrounded Zoe, both of us, and I'm certain the medical team. They had said there was a possibility of death. But Zoe's biblical name says, LIFE! (Editor's note: "Zoe" is the Greek word for *life*.)

A Corporate Worship and Prayer Meeting

Calls were placed, Facebook messages were posted, and emails were sent to inform friends and family that surgery was imminent. Chris asked my dad to gather our family and guests in the chapel for a devotional and prayer.

During Dad's devotional, he explained that God doesn't allow these tribulations to punish us. Our debt was paid with His Son's blood on the cross. My mother has always said that God's ways are higher than our ways, and we can trust that He has a plan in all of this. It was as if an elephant stepped off my back. I wept with relief, confident that my Heavenly Daddy loved me and was *for* me.

Becca Greenwood, my second mother, and spiritual mentor rerouted her trip from Colorado to Germany to get on her knees in Houston and plead for Zoe's life. When she called *United Airlines* to change her flight, prepared to pay the additional $1,000 expense she had been quoted, she was surprised when the operator hearing why she was requesting the change, waived all fees, then stopped and prayed on the phone with her! God's favor was all around us, as the doctors, our family and friends served us.

Within an hour the hospital chapel was filled with loving family and friends. My brother Robert led us in anointed worship, and my mother led us in fervent corporate prayer for almost two hours as the surgeons operated.

It was a difficult challenge for Chris, Zachary and me. In that crowded chapel, through our cascading tears, by faith we claimed God's promises as we worshipped and celebrated His faithfulness. A supernatural peace settled over all of us. Hundreds watched and participated via a Facebook Live video broadcast. Even those who were not at the hospital said they could sense the powerful presence of God during the service.

God gave us prophetic words that night in the chapel. Earlier that day, the doctors had met with Chris, my mom and me, in the conference room. They said that they felt that Zoe would live, but were unsure if she would ever talk, walk, or enjoy quality of life.

Our friends Louis Galvan and Becca had powerful words. In a vision, Louis saw Jesus at the foot of Zoe's surgical table with the fire of His Spirit flowing over her, and so much more. Then Becca felt the Lord say to her that the removal of the AVM was God's plan all along. He would slam the door to death, and to the dread of a possible new brain-bleed. Instead of us grieving over the idea of surgery, this was Zoe's new beginning. They would remove all of the AVM, and she would live and prosper. What had felt like a huge devastating setback, appeared now to be a miracle in the making.

With these words, an anointing to believe swept over us! Joy replaced our tears, and in that worship and prayer time, I felt my first true sense of rest. I could relax. There were watchmen on the wall. My burdens were being carried spiritually and physically to the feet of Jesus. After days of shallow breaths and extreme heaviness, I could finally breathe. I will never forget the love and support shown to us in those dark hours, and the words God spoke to us through people just like us.

The first two of the eight-hour surgery, we had no word. The surgeon had designated a trusted team member to update us via text messages through a secure server. But we weren't receiving updates. I didn't know whether to believe the adage, "No news is good news." Maybe they had a change of plans. Perhaps her body didn't accept the first blood transfusion. She might be experiencing seizures, so commonly associated with an AVM. My thoughts ran wild on an emotional roller-coaster.

Then the first of many updates came through. They "were mapping." For hours, they had strategically mapped her brain, using the various scans they had done, to determine the safest approach to remove the damaged vessels.

After five long hours of surgery, a member of the surgical team thoughtfully came by to tell us he was 99.5% sure they had stopped the bleeding and removed the AVM. *We rejoiced!*

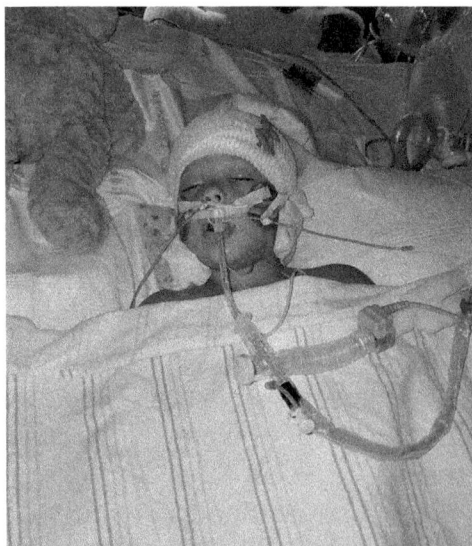

6

SOCIAL MEDIA

Zoe's uncle Robert Smith had created our public Facebook group at: https://facebook.com/groups/pray4zoe so we could both post public updates.

Our family members and extended family members had been the first to sign up. To our surprise, friends began telling friends, and soon comforting messages began to pour in from around the world. One of the first posts was this prayer:

> "Lord, I ask that you heal Zoe. Wrap your healing arms around her, give her the strength to pull through this and get back to being her normal self. Lord, I ask that you give Christopher and Ashlee Morris peace of mind. I know they are going through a lot, and have many questions. Lord, let them know that You are in control and that everything is going to be alright. In Jesus' name, I pray. Amen."

The next day, Chris and I went into Zoe's room and created this video.

http://tinyurl.com/yc8nttzo

*[Publishers note: As of the date of publication, this video
has been viewed more than 50,000 times.]*

With this video, Chris posted the following:

"This is why we're praying. Continue to bless
her, Lord. We can't live without her. Mommy and
Daddy love you so much, Zoe Lee Morris."

Along with this video, here is one
of my favorite photos of Zoe, which I
posted by faith, "You shine bright Zoe
Lee Morris. Sleep well. We continue to
pray for your full recovery." Many who
were carrying our burden had never
even met Zoe. I felt it was important
that we introduce them to her.

As I look back on it now, it's easy
to see how the Lord used the hospital's

remarkable medical team to pull Zoe through her crisis. But, it was the hundreds of precious messages of encouragement and prayers like the one above that pulled Chris, Zach and me through it. We will be forever grateful.

Friends and family began to post encouraging photos and collages of Zoe at happier times, in happier places, like this one, from Aunt Angie (her GG).

Those positive images were so important to us because we were surrounded by nothing but sickness and dying.

A family friend, George Puskas, posted this reminder of Zoe when she was in good health, with her buddy, his son, Brody.

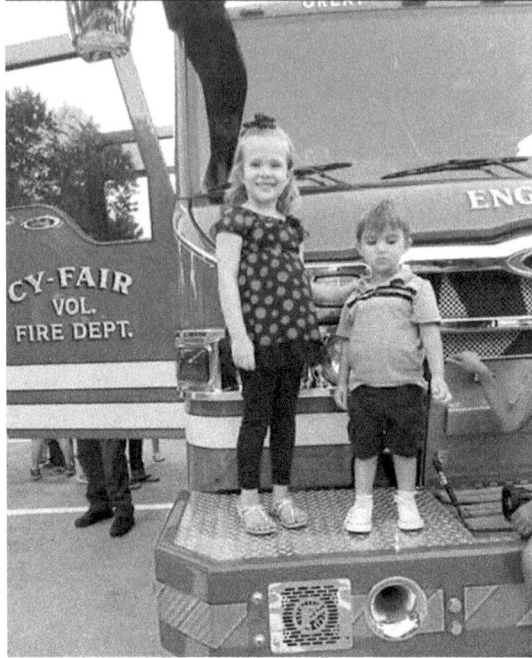

The prayers continued, and many friends posted their written prayers in the Facebook group as well. Many were praying for the doctors, and caregivers who attended to Zoe. They prayed for wisdom, alertness, even for the proper equipment to be available with which to treat her.

Deedee Staggs posted this photo of her beautiful Hadleigh praying for Zoe. She wrote:

> "Hadleigh is praying for her sweet Zoe, with the "boo boo" on her head, to feel better as soon as possible. We love you so much Zoe, Ashlee and Chris. We're praying so hard! ♥"

I'm confident the prayer of a child brings joy to the Father's heart.

Some in the group posted links to encouraging songs, videos, and poems.

Following her lengthy brain surgery, the pressure continued to build in Zoe's brain, and the spikes were again into the danger zone. There was concern that the bleeding might have begun again. A "re-bleed" would demand an additional surgery.

Since we were originally told that surgery was too dangerous to perform, we could hardly bear the thought of a second surgical procedure. After what we'd hoped, and had been told, the emergency surgery was successful, to have to repeat it would be heartbreaking.

Around 6:00 PM, the doctors took Zoe for a second Angiogram to determine if her surgery had or had not been successful, or if she would require a second surgery. Had they completely removed the AVM? Had the bleeding truly stopped? We waited expectantly for the outcome.

Later, we were greatly relieved when the doctors report-ed *there was no sign of further bleeding. The AVM was entirely gone! The scan was clear!*

Now, looking back, I see how the surgery seemed like a setback; but, without it, we would have woke each morning knowing our Zoe had damaged vessels sitting in her brain that could burst at any time. What we had felt was defeat, was in some ways the miracle for which we had prayed.

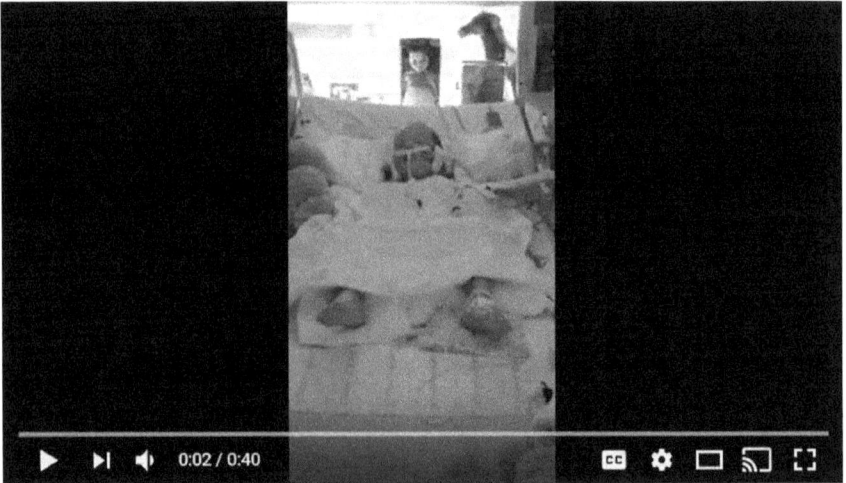

Watch a brief video of Chris talking to Zoe (Day 5)
http://tinyurl.com/y7vf8zjd

Of course, Zoe was still sedated, with breathing tubes in her lungs providing the needed oxygen. She was unable to breathe on her own. She had a feeding tube in one nostril, with multiple IVs that provided nourishment and medication. She was still unconscious in a medically-induced coma.

One night in the ICU I jumped up from a dead sleep, and nearly fell out of bed because of a terrible nightmare that

Zoe was going through seizures. I woke Chris, but instead of concerning him with the dream, I went to the hall outside and called for our amazing night-nurse, Frank. He assured me that according to his video monitor and a dozen machines, Zoe hadn't moved an inch since we left her; literally!

There were moments like this when I had to stand tall in my faith, kick back fear, and not allow it to control me. Under the circumstances, it was so unnatural, but we had to stay rested because when she woke, she'd need us the most.

During this time, a recurring theme from the Facebook messages people posted was God's plan for Zoe's future. When your daughter has been unconscious for days and is even unable to breathe on her own, to be told that she had a future was one of the greatest faith-building gifts we could have received. Many people reported that when they were praying, they sensed that one day Zoe would minister to the nations. One lady said, "She is going to do great things for God!" (To this day, people continue to share with our family their visions and dreams of a ministry they feel Zoe will have one day.)

We usually think of prayer as our speaking to God. However, we've learned that God speaks to those who speak to Him. And He certainly seemed to be doing that. The Bible refers to these as "prophetic words," that God reveals to encourage others.

Another phrase that came up repeatedly was, "Zoe never leaves my thoughts..." "I'm praying continuously..." "what a wonderful testimony she will have." The words varied a bit, but the thoughts were much the same.

Chris asked people in our Facebook group to tell us where they lived. More than 1,000 Facebook friends responded.

People were praying from almost every state in the nation, and from more than a dozen other countries!

The prayers and comments were filled with faith, promise, praise, and gratitude to God. I don't recall one that sounded doubtful, or worried. God's positive people are amazing!

One sweet lady posted:

"Speaking LIFE to her brain, and every cell in her body in Jesus name. Declaring, she is going to sing again. Mercy, Mercy, Mercy, Mercy, Mercy, Mercy, Mercy. Seven times over Zoe's life in Jesus Name!"

I was honestly surprised that so many men "adopted" little Zoe in her struggle. Her dilemma touched even single men. We had been in discussions about adding a pool to our backyard, and the gentleman who assisted us messaged that he'd been praying for Zoe every day.

One lady private messaged me that she was getting her oil changed at *Christian Brothers* and the service writer, our dear friend, Paul, shared his burden for Zoe, so in turn, she was praying. Aside from our blood family, our adopted family of friends carried us many times. We saw several tough guys weep at her bedside in the early days. The men's posts were often tender, and fatherly. Ladies seemed to step into Zoe's issue in motherly ways. One sweet lady posted:

"I stand with you all and agree in prayer that Zoe will awaken with no residual effects of this. That all areas of her brilliant brain, the Father has given her, will function as it is supposed to. That there will be no damage to a single cell! That all blood flow, every artery, vein, every single vessel will have adequate blood flow. That all nerves will be intact. That every thought that she has will be transferred rightly, so and that every word in her speech will be clear. That all of her motor skills will be intact."

Zoe was still unconscious. She was off blood pressure meds, and they had detected no further bleeding. There was, what they called, "hazing" on her lungs, which they were treating.

The doctors were concerned about why her ICP (pressure on her brain) would still spike, from time to time, and then go down. They reminded us that she could likely hear us, but she could not respond in any way. Since the bleeding had stopped, we were encouraged to speak words of comfort and encouragement to her, and to sing over her, songs that she loves. We would often place our phones on her pillow and play her favorite worship songs while she slept peacefully.

Many people offered to come to the hospital to visit her, but at that point, we maintained very limited visitation.

Our immediate goals were to keep the pressure on her brain at low levels. We needed to see her lungs healed to the point that she could breathe, and oxygenate her blood, on her own. Then they would remove the breathing apparatus. We were desperate to see a reduction in her medication; and for her to be free from all the tubes and IV's, and be pain-free. We wanted so badly to know that she was capable of waking up.

Chris posted that night:

"Zoe loves to worship God and sing for Him. We want her healthy and back to normal, so she can continue to do so. Please keep her in your prayers as she continues to fight for her life. Her recovery will be a long process, but we will remain optimistic that she will walk out of this place, and share her testimony to the nations."

7

PEOPLE WANT TO HELP

People continually asked how they could help. Some suggested that we create a "crowdfunding site," which is a website where people could read Zoe's story and contribute to the need as they felt led.

My dad created a "www.GoFundMe.com" page for Zoe's support. We had been so focused on her around the clock care; we had spent little time considering what her situation would demand of us financially.

To this point, Chris and I were unable to work. At least one of us had to be with Zoe continually. She couldn't be left alone. We didn't know how long that would be; how much longer she would be in the hospital; or what on-going post-op therapy might be required. We were laser-focused on seeing our precious Zoe restored to health.

God's amazing people instantly began to contribute. Many of those who did, had never met her, and never will. They were filled with loving support. We couldn't have been more grateful.

Thankfully, most of Zoe's organs were functioning as intended. She was resting peacefully. She hadn't opened her eyes since that awful Monday night at our house. We had received positive words from the doctors, and prophetic words from spiritual mentors; however, they hadn't seen her that night when she lost strength, vision, consciousness, and speech.

Would she ever be the same?

Although the post operative swelling in her face had gone down, and her color had returned, they remained concerned about the brain pressure. It's was the pressure that could damage the brain and the body. So, they attached an EEG (electroencephalogram) machine to check Zoe's electrical brain activity. They wanted to be sure that she wasn't having seizures. Seizures could be catastrophic. After several hours of testing, we were relieved to hear that there were no seizures.

They began to slowly feed Zoe Vanilla *Pediasure*® through the tubes in her nose (directly into her stomach) in hopes of activating her digestive and urinary systems. At first, she regurgitated it, and they had to suction it from her mouth and nose. Poor baby. We could only trust God that this would improve.

It was especially hard for us to see because Zoe *loves* to eat! In fact, we were thankful for the extra candies and carbs she had at Disney World the month before, I suppose it helped keep some meat on her bones in those days without food!

People in our Facebook group were finding, and some were creating memes (colorful, expressive graphics), and posting them on our group site. My brother Robert thoughtfully created the hashtag #PrayForZoe. It seemed clear that God was somehow raising "a prayer army" to battle on our behalf.

This cute graphic was designed around a photo of Zoe at church, the day before her medical emergency.

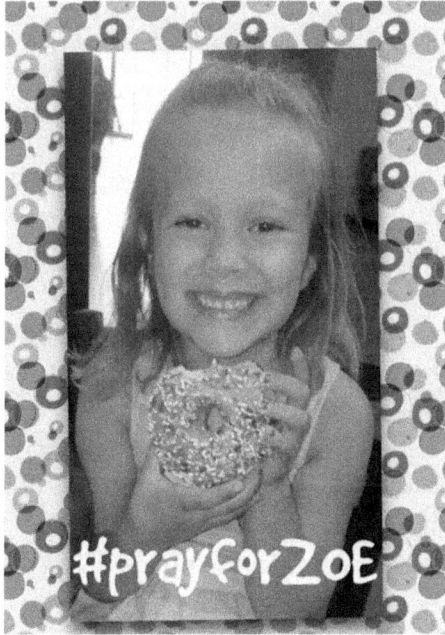

"Sweet precious Zoe, you are adored and loved by so many! We are continuing to pray for complete healing and rejuvenation of your brain. I'm praising God in advance for being able to hear your beautiful voice sing again! Also praying for your amazing family for peace and strength. Love you! ♥"

"Praying for sweet Zoe, I won't stop until she has a full recovery, and even then, she will always be included in our nightly prayers. You're so strong Zoe, so many people love you and we will continue to pray!"

Some comments were quite expressive, some were lengthy, while others were only one or two powerful words, like: "Praying," or "Stay Strong!" Individuals, families, churches, and groups faithfully prayed.

Cynthia Kilgore (Zoe's Nana) posted:

"Zoe Lee—'Life!' (Zoe is the Greek word for 'life.') When your mom and dad gave you that name they had no idea how prophetic it would be in just a few short years. All who know you and those who have heard and responded to your plight, have poured out so much love and praise through Jesus Christ… You have ignited a fire in all who heard the call to pray for you. As God is healing you, He is working through you to spread the good news of saving grace and healing in many hearts, souls, and minds. We all love you so much, Zoe. You are 'LIFE.' ♥"

The next morning, we were relieved to see that Zoe's brain seemed to have stabilized. The pressure remained in the safe zone. They told us that they would likely pull the ICP pressure gauge out of her brain, and close the hole in her head later that day.

Now they could treat her other issues stemming from the brain-bleed more aggressively, and consider lowering the sedation.

8

PNEUMOCOCCAL PNEUMONIA!

We had hardly begun to celebrate our victory when we learned that Zoe had developed pneumococcal pneumonia while on the breathing machine. It seemed our faith was being pushed to the limit—the proverbial "one step forward, two steps back." She wasn't breathing clearly or deeply enough to properly oxygenate her blood. For them to remove the intubation tubes, her lungs would have to be clear. So, they began a procedure to clear her lungs every four hours.

It involved an electric vest that they strapped around her chest. When they turned it on, it would pound her chest for 20 minutes to dislodge mucus in her lungs, which they then suctioned out with a tube. It was quite difficult for me to watch.

One of the more difficult things for us to watch was her withdrawals from the Morphine. She had required a larger dose of Morphine than normal for a child her age. My dad, who worked with drug addicts in the 1960s, said that the withdrawals she experienced coming off Morphine, were reminiscent of those he'd seen with adults coming off street drugs.

Even though she was comatose, at times she would partially wake, suddenly bolt straight up to a seated position, with all the wires and tubes attached; then thrash about wildly flailing her arms and legs. It took two or more strong adults to keep her in the bed. When she settled down, I would hold her and sing softly to her until she fell asleep again.

One afternoon as a nurse was drawing blood Zoe began to punch and kick. I've never been more excited to see my child physically fight. She was moving! Praise God!

Although Chris and I had no way to know what control she would eventually have over her arms and legs, it was clear that she could move them, and she was very strong. Again, these episodes were largely a result of withdrawals from the Morphine. It was horrible to watch her struggle, yet we were encouraged to know that she could *move*. We just wanted our baby back.

Prayer was our breath; our friends were our support, and God was our strength. Many of Zoe's little friends prayed daily for her. Here is Zoe and her friend, Makayla Zuniga.

We issued another prayer alert, for friends to pray that we could get the infection and accompanying fever, under control. The nurses removed the temperature probe, just one of the tubes in Zoe's mouth, into her stomach.

The pressure on her brain, which had kept spiking, and which is one of the more dangerous concerns, had stopped. They removed the pressure gauge that had been inserted into Zoe's brain, and closed with four stitches, which would soon allow us to wake her up.

They removed her catheter.

However, because of pneumonia, the breathing tubes were still in place. We hoped they could remove them soon.

Zoe partially woke the next night, and I sang softly to her. When I paused, she became agitated as if she wanted to say something in return. But with tubes in her nose and down her throat, it was impossible. It must have been quite uncomfortable.

I told her, "Zoe, you are going to be fine. Don't try to speak. We know you love us and we love you. Just let us do the talking for now. We love you and are with you. Just rest." For hours, I laid there singing, "Jesus, Name Above All Names," which was my favorite song as a little girl, and one I'd rocked her to as a baby.

9

BREATH!

Nothing is more necessary than breath. It was God who, when creating Adam, breathed into him the breath of life. We were celebrating the next day. My latest update was at 4:37 AM, when I reported:

> "Zoe just had the clearest x-ray I've seen over these last few days. Her blood oxygen levels are at 100%, and she is comfortable right now. We are on the right track respiratory-wise. Praise God! Thank you, night nurses Frank and Olivia."

We played worship, "It's your breath in our lungs, so we pour out our praise," declaring God's faithfulness to breathe in and through Zoe. Frank, our night nurse, was on duty. He clearly loved Zoe, and we could feel that.

My dad posted:

"We have fought for clear lungs, and for oxygenated blood. Zoe has been receiving periodic lung-clearing treatment that vibrates her chest and loosens phlegm, which they then remove. Her blood oxygen level seems to be holding, for which we are very grateful.

Now we are fighting for:

1. An end to drug withdrawals.

2. Consciousness and recognition of family members.

3. No crippling or mental disabilities. Thank you!

They have administered a med that miraculously removes any memory of these medical procedures. Thank you for praying for Zoe. She is a remarkable gift from God."

My brother Bryan, who's always had a strong prophetic gift, sent us this encouraging message.

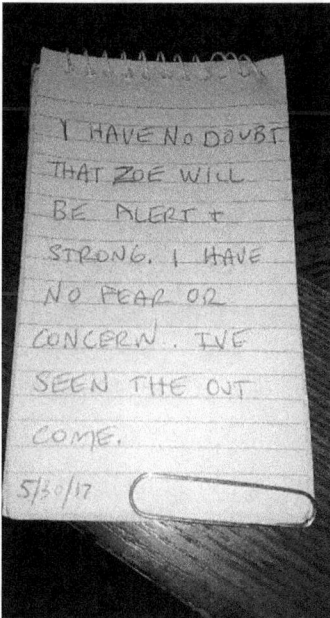

Chris and I anxiously waited to see our baby on the other side. I wanted to see her open her beautiful brown eyes. Would she recognize us? Would she be aware of her surroundings? Would she have memories of all this? Would she be frightened?

We watched as a team of Doctors removed the over-sized intubation tube that had been down her throat for weeks. She began to breathe on her own!

After what seemed like an eternity, she began to shake violently from withdrawals, but her eyes stayed shut. A nurse allowed me to get in the bed with her.

Watch a brief video of this tender moment.
http://tinyurl.com/y9bk4kvg

I jumped into the bed and held her as tight as I could. We laid there as I sang over her for hours. With her waking more and more, we needed to be by her side every minute of every day. Of course, we trusted the staff; but she didn't know them. We waited anxiously for her to show us who she'd be after this life-altering surgery. After all, the last we'd seen her coherent was before bed the night of her ruptured AVM.

The next few days we were able to take Zoe from the bed and hold her.

10

COUSIN TIME &
A SPECIAL GUEST

Interestingly, for whatever reason, the hospital discouraged children from visiting patients in Zoe's condition. Knowing her outgoing, social nature, at this point in Zoe's recovery, we felt having guests near her age would benefit her.

Although we were grateful for Zoe's loving and thoughtful adult visitors, to a childlike Zoe, they seemed to each have an agenda and certain expectations. She felt as if she was being assessed, or challenged.

Children her age, on the other hand, have no agenda or expectations. They just interact, amuse, entertain and enjoy each other. And that, they did.

The next Sunday, my brother Robert, and his wife Missy brought their children River (7 years), and Brooke (5 years) to see her. To be with her cousins was a major blessing.

They brought plastic toy flutes for all. Zoe and Brooke played the flutes, while River conducted. It was a sight and sound to behold. Just five days after brain surgery, she was playing a flute!

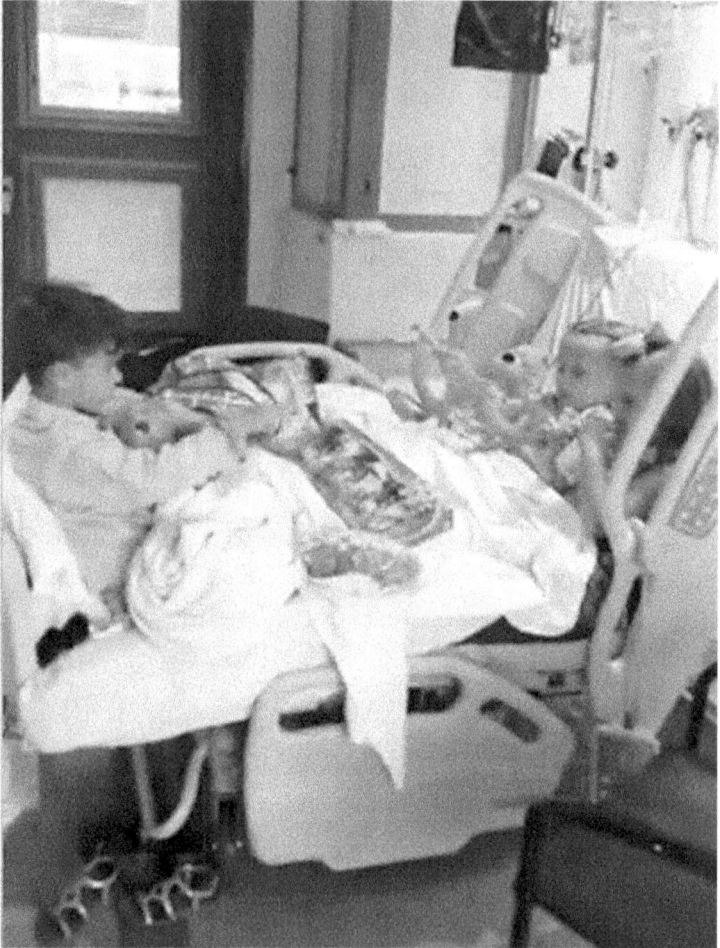

Remember, Zoe is our little musician, who loves to sing worship songs. One of her favorite musicians is the Grammy nominee and three-time Dove Award winner, contemporary Christian singer and songwriter, Kari Jobe. That afternoon, while her cousins were there, Kari made a surprise visit to Zoe via Skype (live Internet video). She encouraged her, sang to her, and sang with her. It was such a blessing. We are so thankful for Kari's sensitivity to our daughter's need.

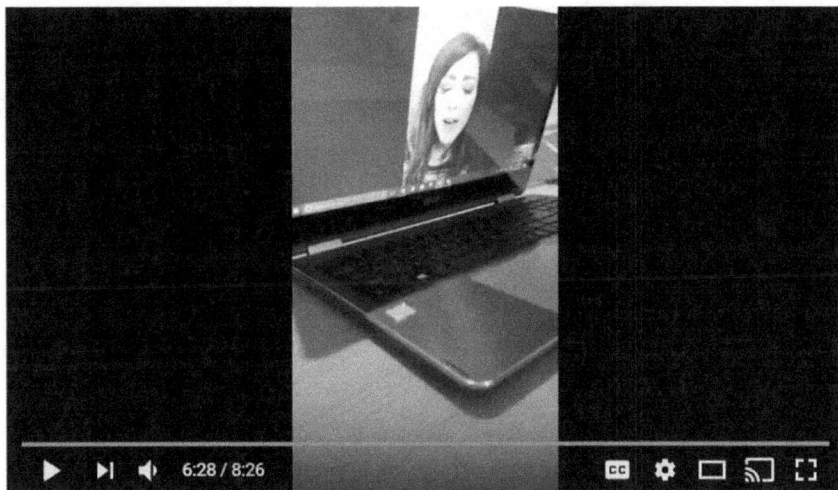

Watch Kari's Skype visit with Zoe, and cousins
River, and Brooke.
http://tinyurl.com/y89shn2o

11

REDUCING ZOE'S MEDICATION

At this point, Chris and I asked the doctors to reduce the amounts of anti-seizure drugs and Methadone. We felt that Zoe wanted to wake up and improve.

We prayed and asked others to pray that she wouldn't have withdrawals and require Methadone again. The doctors were clearly reluctant to reduce the meds because of all she'd been through.

That day they began to reduce the sedatives. At one point, she looked at a nurse and said, "Who are you?" It was a full question! A clearly spoken question with a tad of Zoe Lee sarcasm.

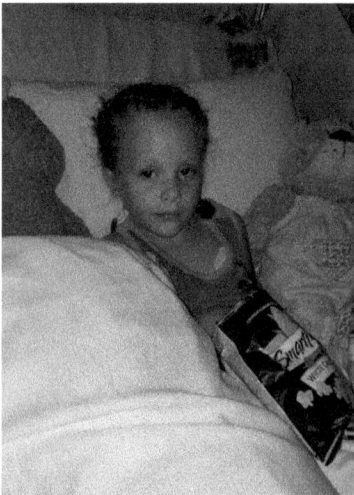

A few days later we were moved up to the PCU (Progressive Care Unit) floor. Although she'd stopped trying to communicate out of her frustration of not being able to form words and sentences, Zoe enjoyed a piece of chocolate, some popcorn, and watched the movie *Pocahontas* that her best friend Olivia had brought. Zoe was regaining her appetite, was more alert, and her vital signs were great. Weaning her off those drugs was, so far, so good.

Still sedated, Zoe slept most of the next day. However, we had aggressively fought to get her meds reduced. The medical team wanted to avoid more withdrawals. Although we understood their concern, she seemed to be frustrated and sad with what little she could do. Chris and I released the staff from liability in the morning rounds. Then we asked them to significantly reduce her medication.

They weren't exactly favorable until a woman appeared who we'd never seen before. She was a middle-aged woman who dressed in street clothes. She did not wear a badge or name tag like the others. However, she seemed to be a person with authority.

She heard our plea, took our side, and stood up for us. She instructed them to reduce Zoe's prescriptions. She approved our request for Zoe to leave the unit, to visit with her cousins and friends in the hall so she could be with children her age. We felt this was vital to our little outgoing, social butterfly's recovery. This lady doctor, who they called "Dr. Gwen," had intervened. She was like an angel, a Godsend to our family. In her first three minutes of meeting us, she had resolved all our concerns.

Throughout the next day, therapists came in and out of Zoe's room. Many left without making any progress. It wasn't necessarily because Zoe was incapable, but because she's so sedated, she could hardly stay awake. I felt sad for her. I so wanted to know who she was under all the medications. Could she hold an idea, initiate a sentence, carry on a conversation? Would she be able to remember the words to her songs? She showed the fight we knew she had, and was ready to be free from the meds, but we struggled to trust the doctors in the process.

By this time, we were more confident that Zoe's lack of speaking, walking, and functioning was largely due to medication. All Chris and I could do was trust God to bring her back to us, and once Zoe's body and mind were clear of those meds, we'd see significant improvements.

That afternoon Zoe's regular doctor made another bold move. He had them skip her Methadone dose altogether. Rather than four doses a day, she would have one a day. God was faithful. Chris and I could hardly wait to see our baby clear-headed and feeling like herself once again.

My dad posted:

"Earth is a battlefield. Isaiah 14:14 explains the battle. It's a battle for who will be worshiped. There, the enemy says, "I will be like the Most High." Interestingly, he realizes that there is a "Most High," something that many humans have yet to realize.

We have sought, through Zoe's experience, not to allow our heavenly Father to be robbed of his praise. Praising Him has been her passion, as well.

As we celebrate His goodness to her, and to us, let's continue to praise Him for her voice and her heart of praise. We know that her heart is to once again express her love for Him."

Later that night I woke to a movement in the bed. I had been sleeping by Zoe's side since the day the nurse allowed me to lay next to her as she came out of the induced coma. When she moved I jerked up and looked over at her. She was lying peacefully, sound asleep with both arms stretched up to the sky. It was like she was having a dream about Jesus calling her, it may have been she was seeing angels, or perhaps she was reaching out to her heavenly Daddy. I knew in my heart that He'd been there with her all along.

12

GOING FOR A STROLL

The next day, with her IV in tow, Zoe's therapist took her out for a walk in the hall. She had not walked more than a few steps since surgery. Zoe is an independent, responsible five-year-old, who cleans her room, makes her bed, dresses herself, sets the table and more. She wasn't used to being incapacitated. She had no idea where she was, or what she had experienced. She was uncomfortable being waited on, though she was still somewhat sedated.

Although she walked amazingly well, having laid flat on her back for nearly three weeks, she had emotional difficulty. She began to experience anxiety and self-doubt after she walked about 30 feet outside her tiny hospital room, and began to cry. Why? No one would ever know. She wasn't herself at that point, but to push through this was part of her journey. She wept for a minute, then refocused and continued. Dad continued to video her. It took everything in me not to cry with her and run to her rescue. I had to stay strong. I fought to be her source of encouragement.

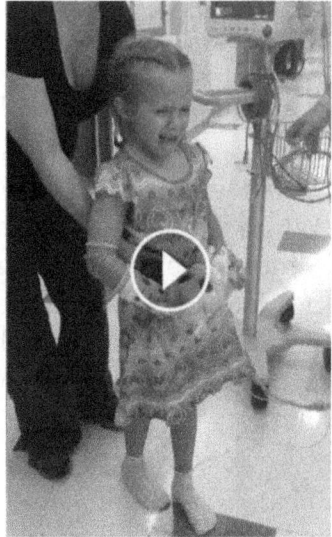

Chris' mother, keeps an excellent photo and video record of Zoe's accomplishments. Here Zoe was, a few months before her trauma, singing one of her favorite worship songs. Nancy posted the video and wrote:

> "She knows him! HE IS GOOD ALL THE TIME, and he is with her right now because HE knows that she trusts him!"

Watch a brief video of Zoe singing "God Is Good."
This was before her surgery:
http://tinyurl.com/ycrkvhhj

A thoughtful partner of mine, Jonas Mancuso, blessed us by sending a *Snow White* look-alike to visit with Zoe. Snow White is one of Zoe's favorite Disney® characters. Remember, a month earlier, during our family vacation at Orlando's Disney World, Zoe had met "the real" Snow White. Now, a beautiful Snow White had dropped by to say "hello," to encourage and chat with her. Zoe was thrilled. Jonas, you are an awesome man!

Watch a brief video of Snow White's visit:
http://tinyurl.com/yb4l6ayq

We were clearly on our way back. However, the next day was hard. Zoe didn't eat, had a fever, refused to try to talk, and threw up all afternoon. We posted another emergency prayer request. It had been 15 days since her brain surgery. They took some cultures and sought to identify the cause of this setback. Zoe felt bad and was emotionally discouraged and confused.

At that point, feeling that perhaps we were pushing her too quickly and expecting too much of her, we asked that almost all visitations stop until further notice, to give Zoe time to process her emotions. She was waking up and having to make many small adjustments that she simply didn't understand.

Our remarkable Facebook friends were holding up our hands, encouraging and supporting us in prayer. Dad said, "Those who say Facebook friends aren't REAL friends, haven't walked in our shoes!"

Wow, it's so true. Chris and I were, and continue to be amazed and grateful, not only for the prayers, and words of encouragement; but also, those who participated so generously with the GoFundMe effort. I'm one who feels best when I give to, or serve others. I prayed that God would abundantly bless those who lovingly supported us.

My mother encouraged us all to ask the Lord, why Zoe kept getting a fever, and vomiting. She posted:

"The doctors don't know why, but God does. Please pray:

1. Pray that any infection in her body will go.

2. Pray that her stomach will be settled, with no more vomiting.

3. Pray that Zoe will have confidence and ability to speak, and to walk totally aware that Jesus is fighting for her.

4. Pray that she will be free to progress to the next level of recovery.

    You are the team. The battle is the Lord's, but we are His warriors who know that this is more than a physical battle. This is spiritual warfare!"

13

MORE PRAISE &
PRAYER MARKS

"Prayer changes things," some say. However, the truth is, "God changes things." Prayer is simply our access to Him. Two things that particularly touch the heart of God are prayer and children. Dad posted these Praise & Prayer points for those who are loving and praying for our sweet Zoe that day.

**Praise...

As posted 30 minutes ago, this morning's MRI scan to test for bleeding in the brain was clear. We are celebrating that result!

**Here Are 10 Prayer Points: Please pray for...

1. Zoe's recurring fever to end

2. her emotional healing

3. her brain to heal flawlessly

4. her to be off all medication

5. her to eat and drink on her own

6. her normal active digestion and urination

7. her speaking to return (surgery was in that area of her brain)

8. a regular room to become available (out of progressive care)

9. in-patient therapy to be available. Texas Children's Hospital (where she is) is the only place that offers it.

10. her remarkable parents, Chris and Ashlee Morris, who are focused on her needs 24/7.

My sister-in-law Missy Smith, Zoe's aunt, posted:

> As I was praying for Zoe this morning and her road to recovery, I realized God had answered a cry of my heart for her. When this tragedy hit Zoe, and we were faced with her life or death, *I asked God to allow me to take another photo of these beautiful cousins smiling and loving on each other.* He's done that… Tears of joy and gratitude… Thank you to all who have sent private messages, posted on Zoe's page, and who have been rock solid support for this family. United prayer has and will continue to move all the bumps in the road that Zoe encounters… She's winning this race and doing it so well. ❤"

Cousin therapy is a good thing.

Top image (Above): Cousin Brooke, Zoe, and cousin River before the incident. Bottom image (Above): Zoe, River, and Brooke in Zoe's bed.

Samantha, Zoe and cousin Gabby enjoy a cone on Zoe's first trip out of her room.

In the early days of ICU our neighbor Gina generously raised money to help with our daily expenses of hospital parking, food, and gasoline for Chris to travel to and from work each day, and spend evenings with us. Gina and her beautiful daughter Jessica came to the hospital with tons of cards and gifts.

They mobilized the entire neighborhood to pray for our family. Gina's a giver and has a great relationship with our local fire department. She shared our prayer request with our local Cy-Fair Fire department. They created an Internet video for Zoe, and prayed for her. It was such a thoughtful gift.

They promoted prayer for Zoe, with signs on their trucks, and in front of their station. It was clear that one of our first stops out of the hospital would have to be the fire station to deliver cookies and to give each of them a hug, which we did. The big sign in front of their unit, which thousands would see as they drove by each day, read: "Pray for Zoe, the Great Eight."

Sometimes a girl's gotta catch a nap! Zoe loved the home-made Super Girl gown that her Aunt Donna made for her, with a matching gown for her teddy bear. We had a picture on her wall that read, "Let her sleep, for when she wakes she will move mountains!" That's just what we did. We continued to monitor visits and protect her down time so she could rest and regain her strength.

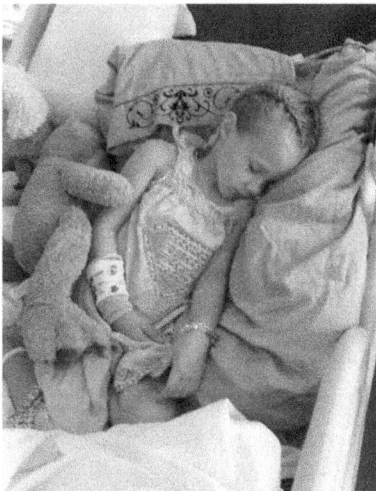

14

FINALLY, OFF ANTI-SEIZURE MEDS & METHADONE!

Meme, Alice Smith, posted the next morning: "Zoe Lee, we are all praying that today will be a great day of victories for you!"

That was a special day for us. Zoe was finally off the Ativan, an anti-seizure medication; and Methadone, the anti-withdrawal medication.

Wow, what a miracle baby! Just a matter of days earlier, our child was in critical, unstable condition. We had no assurance that she would survive, and if she survived, would have what some refer to as "quality of life." GO, GOD! Lord, thank you for showing off!

How do you spell "recovery?"

Eddie, my dad (Zoe's "Pawpaw") spent the day with Zoe and me. He and I took her to get her first haircut and we promised her a special treat while we were out. She was obviously anxious and reluctant to leave the security of her room. She fussed through the washing and cut, but smiled from ear-to-ear with the compliments she received afterward.

Pawpaw took her to the hospital gift shop to pick her treat. He told her that she could have anything in the shop. She chose *Cheetos*®. No, not regular *Cheetos*®. She chose her favorites, "<u>Flaming Hot</u> *Cheetos*®!" Then a large dill pickle to top it off. Dad was hesitant to allow her to get these, but I said, "It's a true test to see if she's her old self. She always loved to eat spicy *Cheetos*® and quickly this became her first meal after surgery!

Gone were the pale, heavily-medicated, emotionless expressions. Once again, we could see the brightness in our Zoe's big beautiful brown eyes and her loving smile. She tried to express herself with simple, single words. However, most of the time there was no sound at all. It was like she was mute.

At other times, the words came out as gibberish and made no sense at all. It was clear that she understood more each day. To conquer her frustration, she began to give us a thumb up for "yes," or a thumb down for "no." Thinking and speaking appeared to be her biggest challenges.

Her amazing big brother, Zachary, made a huge difference. He encouraged her to be silly and not to take things so seriously. Things were emotionally hard for her. She'd always been hard on herself when she disappointed us. Her condition disappointed her, but Zach kept her mood bright.

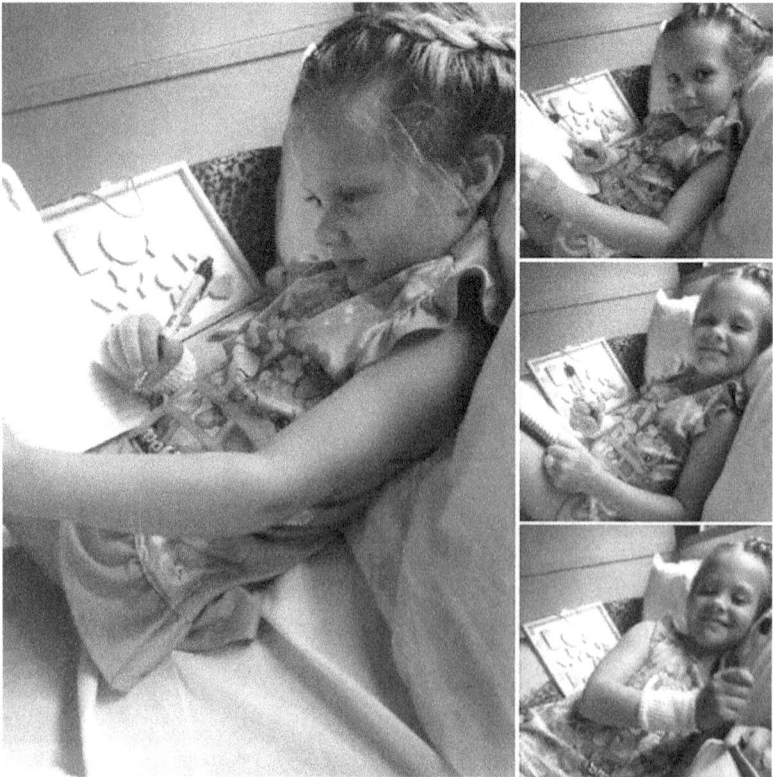

ZOE

My brother Bryan, and sister-in-law Alexa brought their daughter, Zoe's sweet eight-year-old cousin Karmin by for a visit—along with a delicious southern fried chicken dinner for the entire family. All had fun. Zoe struggled to think of certain words, and to speak them; but often, she was only able to stutter a word or two. Sweet Karmin, prepared for that, she was patient and kind to Zoe. She made her feel comfortable.

Uncle Bryan put a balloon under his shirt and pretended to be pregnant. Zoe burst into laughter. He made a big circle with his arms, like a basketball goal, and she threw balloons through it. She loved it. The moment he would stop playing, she'd give him a look. He started to make her say "please," then they would play a few more minutes.

As I watched them play, I began to realize how important good therapy would be for Zoe. In the days past the therapist would come and go with little improvement to speak of. The drugs controlled her emotions, and hindered her ability to move, talk, or think. Many times, because of her frustration to communicate, their visits only caused her to feel defeated and shut down.

That night Zoe was moved to her fourth room—a regular room! When the nurses came to wheel us to the next level, cousin Karmin and Zoe giggled in the bed through the halls and elevators. Her hospital bed looked like a parade float with tons of balloons and stuffed animals galore. Some of her first moments being herself occurred that night. I loved that her joy had returned.

Zoe treasured the many cards and letters our friends had sent her. We had a box of cards and Scriptures that our friend Jill Young had her students write. There were gifts and balloons, books and encouraging words from people all over the nation. As I read them to her, she would see her name in them, even in cursive, and pointed to it with excitement. She tried to speak it, but the word "Zoe" simply wouldn't form. However, we were encouraged to see her recognize her written name, and to know that she could at least make sounds. She mostly struggled with word formation, but we had braced ourselves for no speech at all, and she was trying!

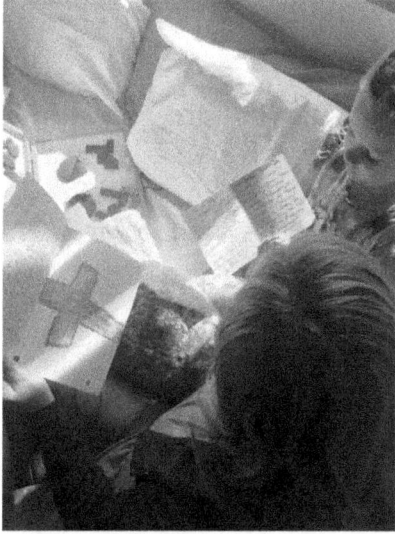

Within the next day or so, Zoe watched a *SnapChat* video she had made with one of her many GG's, Jean, my dear friend who's been a constant help. We were at *Salt Grass Steak House*, enjoying our last dinner with Jean's mom, who died a month later. Zoe and GG made a video. She put the panda face on it and said, "I'm a Panda, I'm a Panda." As she watched the silly video of herself, she'd made the month before, she began to say softly, but bravely, under her breath, "I'm a Panda." <smile>

God was teaching us to focus gratitude on even the smallest positive things we could see, rather than on the negative things that appeared.

It had been a few weeks since we had rushed our precious daughter to this hospital. Partly due to our insistence, they had now stopped giving her Methadone and Ativan. To my untrained eye, her issues seemed to be the ability for her to think the right thoughts, to form them into words, and to speak them. We had faith that those things would come in time, since we'd been told that children's brains are quite pliable and can reconstruct remarkably well.

Our thanks to all who sent us inspiring notes, cards, art-work, and financial support. We might have lost our daughter had they not picked up the assignment to intercede, war, and to stand in the gap through prayer for her.

15

COMPLETE SENTENCES

Zoe loves God. She delights to sing heartfelt worship songs to Him. She also loves to pray. She is a very spiritual five-year-old. In this photo, my mother, Alice Smith prayed for Zoe, at a church altar, months before her crisis.

You may recall the Monday night when we were woken up by Zoe's screams. What I didn't mention was that night, as every night, we gathered around her bed for bedtime prayer. Being the youngest, she typically prayed last. So, the last words we heard Zoe speak before she became comatose were her prayer, "Thank you God for my mommy and my daddy…"

That first night of her being drug-free and in her new room, we gathered around her bed and prayed for her, taking turns as we do at home. When we finished, to our surprise, she spontaneously prayed aloud—*in complete sentences!*

She quietly stuttered the words, "Dear Lord, thank you for this day, thank you for mommy and daddy. Amen." Chris is my witness, I'd never heard a sweeter prayer. This was Zoe's miracle; she's was getting past the meds and coming back to us.

As it should be, Zoe's last words before, and her first spoken sentence following her brain surgery was a prayer. *Thank you, Jesus!*

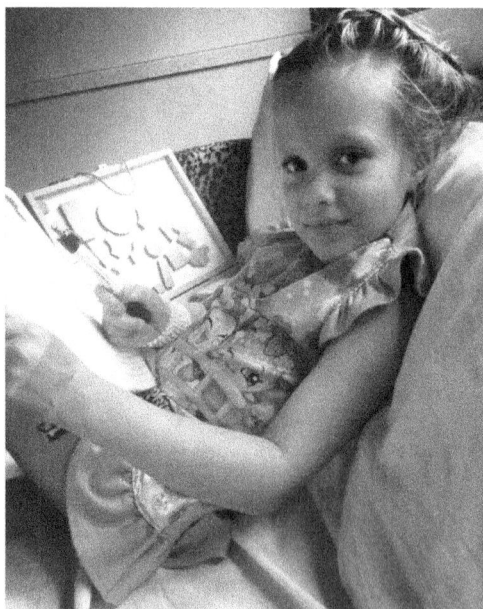

Zoe has an abundance of "grandmas." The next day, her Grandma Val came by for a visit. She had created some beautiful beaded bracelets to remind people to pray for, and to support Zoe. The proceeds from their sale would go to Zoe's support fund. The accompanying descriptive brochure she had created said:

ZOE

"ZOE'S BRACELET

The 28 glass pearls in this bracelet represent Ephesians 2:8, 'For it is by grace you have been saved. Through faith – and this is not from yourselves. It is the gift of God.'

The 88 metal beads represent Matthew 8:8, 'The centurion replied, "Lord, I do not deserve to have you under my roof. But just say the word, and my servant will be healed."

This bracelet was designed for Zoe Lee Morris by her grandmother, Valeri Morris.

The entire Morris family is a Christ-centered and Christ-led family.

We know and believe that the thousands of prayers prayed for Zoe have had a huge impact on the healing that she has received and the healing yet to come.

Psalm 37:4 says: *'Delight in the Lord and He will give you the desires of your heart.'*

It is the earnest desire of our hearts that Zoe will have complete healing and, believing that God's Word speaks only truth, we WILL delight in Him, even during this difficult season.

James 1:12 says: *'Blessed is the one who perseveres under trial, having stood the test, that person will receive the crown of life that the Lord has promised to those who love Him.'*

We, as a family, not just of blood, but of Christ, will stand firm under this trial, believing our God is a God of miracles and healing.

Again, we appreciate our friends so much. You have lifted us up in prayer and spirit. We love all of you for your love and support in this very challenging time."

Val, I love you dearly and will hold this special bracelet in my heart forever. Thank you for honoring our Lord and Zoe's life in such a meaningful way.

That day, the staff permitted me to take Zoe for a stroll outside to a hospital garden. It was the first sunshine that she'd seen and felt in three weeks. God is good!

We had our first dinner together as a family since Zoe's AVM bleed. Zach had visited Zoe many times before, but she had always been medicated and sleeping. That evening at one point, he had to excuse himself from the table in tears. He loves her so much and was shocked by the sister that he was seeing. He said he just hoped she would be back to normal soon. While people around us saw much progress, we knew there was a long road ahead.

We asked our Facebook friends to pray for these three things.

1) Pray that Zach's time with Zoe would encourage them both and that they would enjoy this night together. We have missed him terribly.

2) Pray for a room to open for our next step, which was therapy, on the twelfth floor. She could require weeks of inpatient therapy at TCH. There were only three such units in the

State of Texas, one in the City of Houston, which only had eight beds. We would need divine favor for this.

3) Pray for continued healing, emotional and physical strength, and for the courage and ability to speak. ♥

The next day, Dad posted:

> "Today our precious Zoe's emotions were all over the board. Many smiles, much weeping. Pray today for the healing of her *mind*, as well as her *brain*.
>
> It's important that we remember that the mind and the brain are not synonymous. For children, I describe the brain as the bicycle the mind rides.
>
> If the brain is broken, the mind is hindered. Zoe's brain trauma affects her mental state. Her brain is still in the healing process.
>
> Let's thank the Father in advance for the wonderful work of healing He is performing in her for His glory; and for His peace to rest upon her in the process."

That night got scary. It was rough. Zoe could not settle down. Her pupils were dilated, and she continually giggled and laughed for little or no reason. The day before, she had cried all day. Her extreme emotions were bizarre and hard for us to watch. We almost had to revert to Methadone; but thankfully, with God's natural essential oils[1] and Melatonin she finally fell asleep.

Zoe has loved essential oils since birth. What we share regarding our experience is not to suggest oils instead of medication.

Her blood pressure had been high, which was a concern we were watching closely. They had weaned her off all but Clonidine, which was administered to regulate her blood pressure.

The next day we were told that a 12th-Floor therapy room would be available in a day or two because a patient was to be discharged. Zoe was first on the list!

One of my favorite Bible passages is Philippians 4:6-7, ESV, where God says,

"Do not be anxious about anything, but in everything by prayer and supplication with thanksgiving let your requests be made known to God. And the peace of God, which surpasses all understanding, will guard your hearts and your minds in Christ Jesus."

That night was the third night that Zoe had quietly prayed, with a bit of stuttering, without being prompted. However, she was so anxious to pray as we tucked her in, she interrupted my prayer. Honestly, I couldn't have been more delighted!

I mentioned that to my dad the next day. He said he wasn't surprised. "Ashlee, Zoe doesn't hesitate to pray because she's addressing the One with whom she feels the most comfortable."

It was so simple, yet so true. We, Zoe's parents, her grandparents, aunts, uncles, friends, doctors, and therapists could prompt her to speak all day long, but she preferred to talk to her Heavenly Daddy. With Him, there was no pressure, concern, or expectation. She was at total peace—just her and God.

Oh sure, we had our daily struggles, both with Zoe and ourselves. But we were consistently reminded how awesome this miracle was, and how blessed we were to have witnessed it.

Zoe's "Meme," my mother, Alice posted,

"I realize today, when I visited Zoe, that she is now very aware of her limitations. Even though she smiles and tries to appear okay, in her little five-year-old heart, I can see her frustration with not being able to communicate as she wants.

Prayer leader and friend, Becca Greenwood, was with me today. When Becca prayed and thanked Jesus that Zoe will sing again, Zoe wept quietly. Her reality and her vision are not the same. But your prayers are allowing the supernatural move of God to transcend and supersede the natural. Thank you for believing with us. The unseen will be seen—soon!"

The next day, Mom posted:

"Today I played an improvised "color game" with M&M candy. (I'm such a scheming Meme.) Zoe loved the game and pronounced the colors after me. The sad part is, unless I would say the color, she didn't know what it was. But every step has been such a miracle along the way.

Ashlee was washing clothes, and I was sitting in Zoe's room while she was napping. We had worship music on. Suddenly, while listening to a moving song, in her sleep, she began to cry.

I believe the Lord was privately ministering to her even in her sleep. I almost lost it watching that. I talked to her about the nations and how I go to preach in nations and she wept like she knew every person in each nation. OMG, I am experiencing a personal revival just watching this baby. Amazing God..."

For my lady readers, especially, who know how important it is to feel pretty, here is Zoe's huge battle scar, above and behind her left ear. I am so glad our surgeon was a woman! Doctor Lam was very conservative. You'd never know Zoe had undergone brain surgery. Virtually nothing was shaved, and her hair naturally covers the scar. (I've highlighted it in white.)

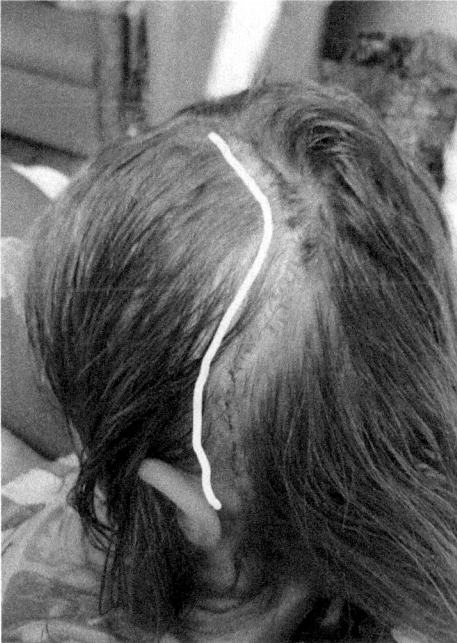

She also has four stitches to the front of her head where the pressure gauge had been removed. Plus, four stitches in her upper thigh where a central IV line was attached, along with one stitch on each wrist.

16

OUR "BUTTERFLY" EMERGES FROM HER COCOON

That night, during bedtime prayers, Zoe showed her appreciation for the beautiful mermaid blanket sent to her by a work partner, Kathy Ried.

It was amazing to me that she had gone through so much, but remained so grateful and kind. When we lay together in her hospital bed, she'd often tickle my back and tell me how much she loved me and worked to encourage me. She will make such a good mommy one day.

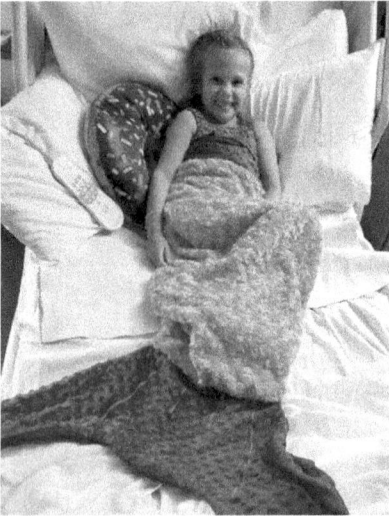

She's wise beyond her years, and she loves with a mother's heart. Her graciousness rubbed off on the doctors and nurses. They often came in quiet and tired, but left grinning from ear to ear. She's thoughtful, sweet and brings joy into most every situation. It's no wonder our nurses felt their "Sunshine" was leaving, when we left.

Dad spent the next day with us, and posted:

"Zoe was so sweet today. With all the nurses interrupting her, docs checking on her, and more, not one tear, no complaints, no whining, simply her usual kind and happy demeanor. She smiled, giggled and laughed. Still quieter than usual. But so pleasant and cooperative. God's grace is all over her. Our 'little butterfly' has exited the cocoon. She's simply getting her wings now. (James 1:17)"

We had our first psychological testing the next day, and learned that sweet Zoe was having issues with left brain/right brain coordination, short term memory, her ability to match items, and to recognize colors (she once knew). She's very bright, but "the contents" had been jumbled with her brain-bleed and traumatic surgery.

The doctors seemed pleased, but explained that there was significant ground to regain through therapy. A wonderful speech therapist began to work with her.

Zoe loves to sing, and she responds best to music. However, it took 30 minutes or longer before she was willing to attempt to speak to the therapist. She was quite self-conscious, and ill at ease. After that, she warmed up and began to sing the alphabet song entirely. She spoke one or two words at a time. Then she counted to 10 with the doctor in English, and again in Spanish with us. She remembered certain things.

The neuropsychologists (therapists) explained concern for her short-term memory, as in, "I showed you a kitty five minutes ago. You watched me hide her here in the room. Where is the kitty now?" She couldn't remember what she had just seen. She also had difficulty matching physical objects with picture representations.

That night, Dad encouraged me to write this book about our journey, to document what God was doing and to share what we'd learned of God's goodness and the love of His people. He felt it would possibly benefit other parents who face similar challenges.

Here is one of my favorite photos of Zoe. Dad was trying to get her to smile for the camera, but she was about to burst a dimple to avoid smiling. :) She was wearing a special hand-made AVM Awareness necklace from Hanna O'Neil.

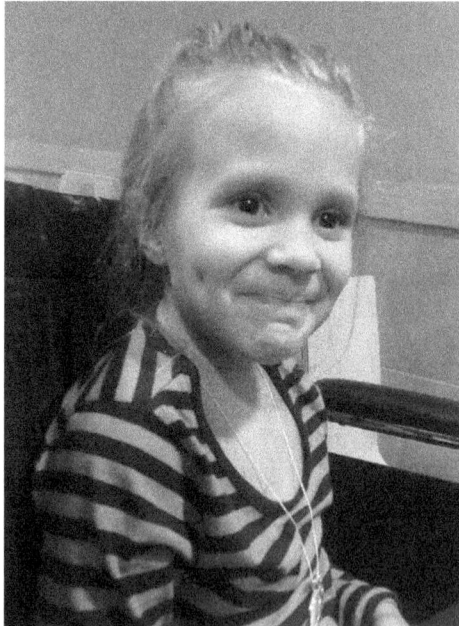

Zoe's number one boyfriend is still her brother, Zachary, ten years her senior. She adores him, and he adores her. He is the most patient, kind and supportive big brother, I've ever known. We are so proud of him. Since the beginning, he spent countless hours in the hospital with us, day and night, always showing strength and encouraging Zoe to laugh, play and remain lighthearted.

She felt safe with Zach, she knew he wasn't judging her with expectations, he loved her as she was and wouldn't push too much. I am incredibly proud to be Zachary's mother. I couldn't imagine this journey without him. He's been patient, caring, sensitive, yet strong.

We continued to pray for Zoe:

1) Her continued strength

2) Her courage to speak more and more

3) Her to regain her short-term memory

4) Her not to be discouraged in the therapy setting

The next day, Chris began driving 45-minutes to an hour, to and from the hospital each day for work; then often showing homes to his real estate clients in the evening before he returned. He was (and is at the time of this writing) an Intranet technician and a Keller Williams® realtor. I am proud of and grateful for him. What a remarkable man, husband, and father he is.

The long work hours and commute must've been taxing at times, but he pushed through. He often returned to the hospital in the evenings and commented on the progress he saw. Perhaps because I never left her side I couldn't see the progress as clearly as he could. I was so close to the situation, it was hard for me to see that we were reaching small goals. My husband lovingly shared new perspective, and offered new hope. Where I'd feel discouraged about her having lost her ability to recognize her colors, and her inability to remember simple words, Chris saw the larger picture and would share improvements he saw.

I was doing my best to balance my jobs, with Zoe's therapies, and doctor's appointments. I quickly learned that to be a patient's mother is a full-time job by itself! However, I was also a full-time RE/MAX® realtor; the Executive Assistant for my parent's ministry, the U.S. Prayer Center; and the property manager of

www.TexasRiverCondo.com.

Finally, the approval came and a room became available for us in the Therapy Unit on the Twelfth Floor. This was a God-ordained approval. Zoe was one of 12 patients waiting for that room. This hospital is only one of two in the state that offer this level of inpatient therapy. We were blessed!

The therapists began working with Zoe. Her walking and speech had been affected by the brain trauma. We believed it would be turned around for the glory of God, but we were aware of the intense need for continued support.

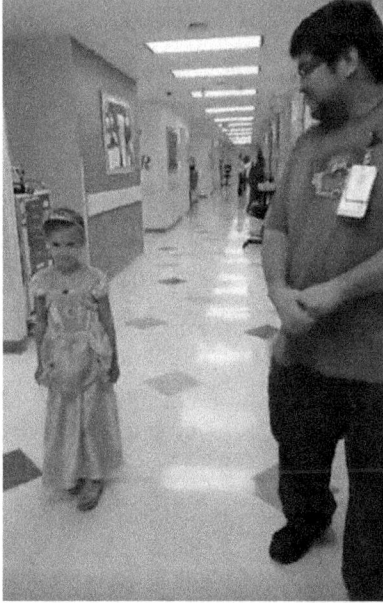

Watch a brief video of Zoe and Physical Therapist Edwardo.

http://tinyurl.com/yb4o9e4d

Mother posted that day:

"As I reflected tonight about the past 21 days of Zoe's medical emergency, there are no words to express our gratitude to each of you Facebook friends. You are the best, and I pray for a rich abundance of God's grace and provision to be given you. Thank you, thank you. Zoe still needs a lot of healing, but wow, the Lord has performed mighty miracles thus far. I know that your prayers and support continue to make a difference!"

Throughout this journey, I had not allowed myself the time to think about house and home. It didn't seem profitable to me to wishfully think about the things I missed, but now that we were on the 12th and final floor of our hospital stay, I could see the light at the end of the tunnel. Soon, we'd be back in our own home.

One night, I cried myself to sleep thinking about how far we'd come, but wondering how I'd handle it all when we returned home. So much had changed. Our brave little girl who knew neighborhood and street safety often played outside until the streetlights came on, and jumped freely on the trampoline in our back yard for hours. She would not be allowed to do many of her favorite things, there was still so much to navigate on her road to recovery. It was scary to think about handling all the therapy and changes on my own, but little did I know that a blanket of friend and family support waited for me on the outside.

ZOE's "Therapists for the Day."

Cousin's River and Brooke, Robert and Missy's youngest children, returned to love on, entertain, and to challenge Zoe the next day. Pictured below, cousin River, Zoe, and cousin Brooke gazed out the 12th-floor hospital window. We finally had a room with grass and trees outside. Before, we looked at a sea of big tall buildings, AKA the Houston Medical Center.

We were thankful that Aunt Missy brought her "therapy crew" to see us. I was finally able to envision the fun those three, with cousin Karmin, would have on our family's summer vacation on the dude ranch, which was less than a month away. We had goals, for the first time in over a month. The future was within reach.

In our new room, we spent long days with various therapists. Our days were filled with speech therapy, occupational therapy, physical therapy, music therapy and more, filled our days. Doctors continuously interviewed us about Zoe. Some of those questions brought me to tears, especially those tough questions asking me to compare her "before the incident" with her "right now." But I know the professionals needed answers.

One hard question was how she felt about herself before her AVM. She'd been insecure at times during therapy. So, they needed to compare that with her prior emotions. I told them how Zoe was feeding our dog, Sophie. When she pulled the dog food off the shelf, she accidentally knocked my crock pot off as well, shattering the glass lid. I was upset, but Zoe was much harder on herself for disappointing me. She burst into tears.

The doctors I was with saw my tears as I told them the story. My heart was breaking as I thought about how my reaction had caused Zoe such sincere sadness.

The doctors, who were mothers themselves, assured me that Zoe would be fine, that she was hard on herself just as I was hard on myself, but we would have time to grow together and move past this. I constantly had to face times like that, sharing about who she was would often bring high emotions. I wondered if I'd ever get her back to the girl she was before, but I was incredibly grateful to God for sparing her life.

They said they felt that who she was now was closer to who she'd been before the event, compared to other children who had experienced the same; but that there were no guarantees that she'd ever be the same.

They were pleased with Zoe's progress. They said she was far beyond what they had expected. After all, she was alive! She could walk, talk, and express her emotions.

Zoe's neurological team and I noticed that her eyes and brain seemed to have a slight disconnect much like her speech and cognition. Routine things were simple, but to receive, understand, and implement simple instructions seemed to confuse her. There was a delay. In some cases, though she obviously knew the answer to a question, she couldn't process and state it vocally.

We continued to pray for the connections in her brain to realign, strengthen, and to heal. At our request, they tested her vision and hearing. Thank God, she passed both tests!

Zoe talked more and more each day. She sang, laughed, giggled, and painted. She was doing things they didn't expect she'd ever do! We loved her doctors, nurses, and therapists.

One doctor came in after all the assessments and had Zoe walk. He told me that she needed assistance for walking. I politely declined. She was relearning to balance, but could climb stairs with guidance, and could follow a line of colored floor tiles down the hospital halls. Soon she was walking like a pro!

Chris and I support a Ugandan teenager named Jo Ann. We pray for her and pay her way to school. However, because of Zoe's incident, we overlooked Jo Ann's school payment, and sadly she was expelled. When we heard about it, we immediately reached out to the prayer network for Zoe. The request wasn't for Zoe, but for Jo Ann. We were burdened for her, and our partners were happy to cover us in prayer. We wired a payment, prayed, and rejoiced to hear that the school reinstated her. To us, it was just another miracle from the Father. We saw

His faithfulness in every area of our lives.

In a hospital setting, it's easy to become discouraged. However, the next morning our little optimistic Zoe greeted me with a big sweet smile. I fed her breakfast and showed her the "Pray for Zoe" arm bands Chris had produced as a constant reminder to pray. I asked her what color it was. She proudly answered, "blue." The bracelet was red. My heart fell to my stomach.

Then later that day we went to therapy where she rightly answered the difference between hot and cold, pointy or soft touches to every part of the right side of her body.

Although at one time the doctors had not been sure she would ever be able to use the right side again, she had no problem whatsoever. I chose to rejoice that her body was intact. We could relearn colors, but *the feeling* was there! Her nerves were responding.

By the way, as I journaled this report, I was about to write my concern over Zoe's loss of her memory of colors. However, I was interrupted by princess Zoe throwing socks at my head, laughing and giggling. God was faithful to us every step of the way.

Our "butterfly" was emerging from her cocoon. Here she is showing off the swimsuit cover that Aunt Julia gave her in the hospital.

17

CELEBRATING OUR WEDDING ANNIVERSARY

The next day, Chris and I celebrated our 11th Wedding Anniversary. Below is a photo from the previous year.

I'll be the first to admit marriage, even the best marriage, is a roller coaster! When the preacher says, "… for better or worse," he knows there will be good times and bad. There have been times we wanted to give up, when it seemed easier to quit, but we endured. Because of this, God honored us in our weakest moment by giving us the unique ability to strengthen each other.

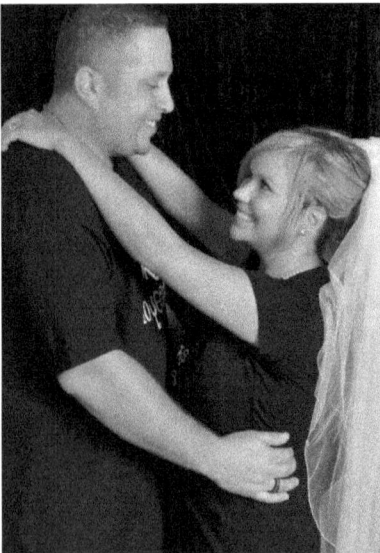

I've never seen the raw emotions of my husband's heart as I did in those mornings of uncertainty. Who would think a marriage could be strengthened by an emergency brain surgery that left our child so close to death. God has been faithful to sharpen us along the way.

Anniversary gifts? Who needed them? We were witnessing the greatest gift anyone could have given us, the gift of Zoe – Life!

ZOE

My mother, Alice stayed overnight at the hospital with
Zoe to allow Chris and me a chance to get away and celebrate
our special day. It was my first night away from the hospital in
almost four weeks! I felt as though I too was emerging from my
cocoon. I cried as we left the hospital. I tried to hold it in but
we weren't even at the elevator before my honey turned to ask
what was wrong.

I trusted my mother, of course, but hadn't been away
from Zoe since the incident. I had no idea what Chris had
planned, but I was glad I could spend time alone with him and
not have to worry about constant vital checks or having to explain our every move to the next person on staff.

Meme and Zoe did well. They played and read books,
took selfies and ate snacks. Meme brought her a very special
gift, a pink opal heart with a diamond necklace. Zoe earned that
gorgeous diamond!

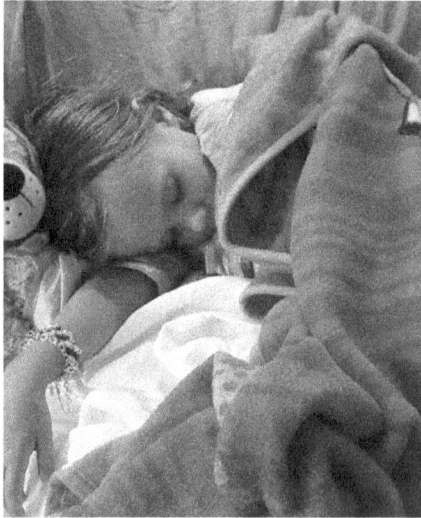

There are few things as precious as a sleeping baby. One doctor commented on how fancy Zoe was to sleep in her jewelry. <smile> Her "Zoe bracelet" rarely came off!

The next morning Mother posted:

"I want to share an experience that happened last night here at the hospital. I stayed with Zoe so her mommy and daddy, Ashlee and Chris, could celebrate their anniversary. Frances, a delightful Jamaican nurse came in Zoe's room around 9:30 PM. She announced, out of the blue, that she knows by looking at Zoe that she has a calling on her life.

Then Frances began to sing, the old chorus, 'What a mighty God we serve,' and the relatively new worship chorus, 'Good, Good Father.' I joined in and began to sing with her. Zoe just stared at her as the nurse danced joyfully around this hospital room. Hmm, this kind of thing keeps happening. Wow, wow and wow."

One of Zoe's favorite songs to sing is "Good, Good Father." However, "What a Mighty God We Serve," was new to her. She didn't quite "nail the lyrics." Instead of "...God we serve," Zoe sang, "What a mighty God *deserve*." <smile> I am certain it made no difference at all to Him! We know that He is drawn to and abides in the praises of His people. (Psalm 22:3) More than once, people expressed feeling the presence of the Lord in Zoe's room(s).

Watch a brief video of Zoe singing, *What A Mighty God DEserve:*
http://tinyurl.com/y9ksc8zg

On our "anniversary get away," my honey surprised me with a pampered pedicure, gorgeous red roses, and a suite on the top floor of the Hyatt Regency Hotel downtown.

As we entered our beautiful room the bellman, an older Indian gentleman about my height, asked where we were from. I explained that we lived in Houston, but were there because our baby was at Texas Children's Hospital. I asked if he prayed, and requested that he pray for Zoe. I cried, he hugged me, I tipped him above and beyond, mostly for the hug! <smile>

Thirty minutes later he called our room to share that his wife was very spiritual, and she told him she felt Zoe would be healed and fully restored.

We received encouragement like that from complete strangers every day. We hung up the phone and wept together, out of gratitude for all God was doing. For the very first time Chris and I could privately share our feelings and bring encouragement to each other.

Zoe and her daddy adore each other.

Zoe's daddy, Chris, was by Zoe's side through the entire ordeal of her AVM. When she woke us that night at the house, screaming in pain, he worked quickly to get her to the nearest emergency room. It's because of his fatherly instinct, wisdom, and fast decision making that she's alive today, and that her quality of life has not been altered further. He's a wonderful daddy.

Although we couldn't leave the hospital, we enjoyed celebrating him on Father's Day. We played Candy Land, and had a picnic on the third floor.

For Chris to see Zoe's smile was the very best Father's Day gift he could get. God had graciously closed death's door for her four weeks previously. It had been a long, hard journey for all involved. Zoe continued to relearn things via therapy.

Zoe walked up to me that day and excitedly said, "Mom!... Umm, umm, umm, I forgot," then graciously laughed and turned to walk away, but not before I grabbed her for a hug of course. She was eager to talk, but the words weren't always there. Sometimes the words were there, but we didn't quite understand what she was trying to say. Then there are times of complete clarity, typically seen with songs, or her silly play talk which required little thought.

When the nurse asked if she needed anything. She said, "Yes." But had nothing she needed in mind. It frustrated her, but she never complained.

I wanted to share our story in hopes of bringing encouragement to others in their times of despair, also to honor the Lord and Zoe's fight for life. I have relayed both the negative, and the positive aspects of our experience. We are beyond grateful to have our baby healthy and alive! Chris and I chose to be transparent during these critical days of Zoe's healing process to provide praise reports and prayer points for more than 6,000 members of our Facebook group, and the many who contributed to our www.GoFundMe.com account.

We also felt that one day our experience might bless and encourage another parent faced with a similar challenge. We know that someday Zoe will read and understand what she experienced, how much we loved her, and how her experience impacted thousands of people around the world.

Her beautiful princess-warrior shirt was made
as a gift to her from our lovely neighbor Gina Pirie

18

DISCHARGED FROM THE HOSPITAL

We were happy to be headed home. It'd been a month since I'd seen my house. Zoe was ready to be home with her puppy, Sophie. Toward the end, she had begun to realize what she'd missed being in the hospital, and asked us every day when we could go home.

One night when she asked to leave, Zach and I explained to her that we couldn't leave until the doctors said we could. She saw the picture clearly that night. She burst into tears and felt homesick for the first time. It was heartbreaking to see her so upset, yet amazing to see her able to process what we'd explained and to feel and express her true emotions.

One of our absolute surprises was the day we were leaving the hospital. Our neurosurgeon, Dr. Sandi Lam, who had performed Zoe's successful surgery, dropped by to tell her goodbye. Dr. Lam had seen her at the elevator a week before and couldn't believe her eyes. She seemed delighted by her work and Zoe's great strides to recovery.

Zoe delivered a special toy to each child in her 12th-floor therapy unit before we left. She signed her name on every card to encourage them. We'd been blessed by each of them, and were delighted to give back and bring a smile to their faces.

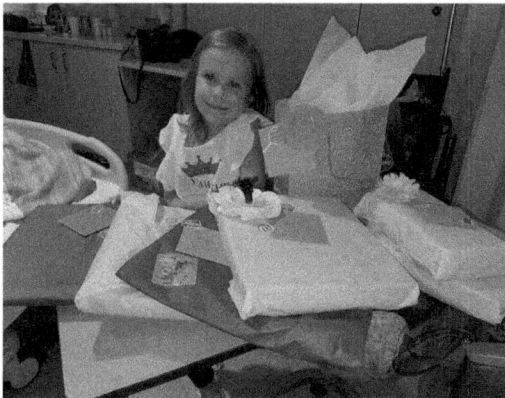

Sarah (pictured below) was the oldest girl in the unit. She worked very hard every day. We never heard her complain, although some of her therapy was quite painful.

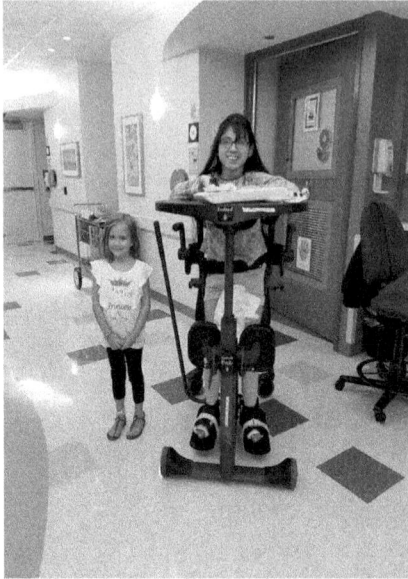

We were thrilled to see one of our sweet caregivers, Frank our night nurse (Below), who was such a comfort to Chris and me during our awful first days in ICU.

You may recall the mysterious woman, mentioned in Chapter Eleven, who appeared and lovingly took command of our situation regarding the reduction of Zoe's medications. We were blessed to thank Dr. Gwen before we left.

Then there was Joseph Harwood, who was Zoe's #1 transportation guy, a believer who encouraged and prayed for us. He helped load us and our things in the car to leave the hospital. Joseph has continued to pray for Zoe and served us in one of our trips when we went back to deliver gifts to parents of the children in ICU,

Zoe's first desire as we left the hospital was for food at Aunt Julia's *Fusion Taco* restaurant on N. Main Street, in the Heights. So, my dad, Pawpaw, took us by, for a delicious meal. As soon as Zoe saw Aunt Julie she asked for a pair of scissors. That seemed like a strange request for a five-year-old who has just left the hospital.

Not at all. Zoe was free and ready to cut off all the ankle bracelets that identified her as an AVM, brain surgery patient. We were done! *Thank you, sister. Your thoughtfulness during our family's time of need means the world to me.*

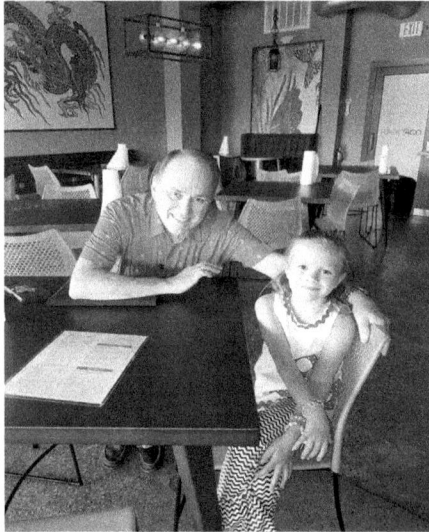

After lunch, we dropped by *Open Door Therapy Center*, in NW Houston, where Zoe would be receiving therapy four days a week. They were quite gracious to schedule us for all phases of Zoe's ongoing treatment.

The therapists, hearing us refer to Zoe as "princess," and seeing photos of her on our Facebook page, with her crown, met her at their office door, each wearing a crown. They graciously greeted us with balloons, hugs, and smiles; then gave us a tour of their facility.

The owners had tears in their eyes as they shared how they'd been following our story. These ladies are mothers with daughters, I could tell they truly felt my heart. They had scheduled every session recommended by the hospital staff to accommodate our every need. They were diffusing Zoe's favorite essential oils which brought us a sense of confirmation, but more importantly, Zoe was at ease. I could see peace over my baby, she was encouraged to meet new friends and not at all fearful about what was to come. I knew that "Open Door" was God's gift for our family. Since that day they've been a tremendous blessing to me.

After that, we made a surprise stop at daddy's office, *Villa Sport – Cypress*, to give him a hug, and to thank those who work there for praying for us. The staff had graciously filled in to allow Chris to be by Zoe's side day and night for three full weeks.

As we entered our neighborhood we saw home after home with yard signs that read: #**PrayForZoe**. Her name and prayer request were posted throughout our neighborhood! She was amazed to see all the people who loved and supported her.

Our yard was flooded with signs to welcome Zoe home. "You've got this Zoe. We love you. Fight like a Zoe. 'I can do all things through Christ who strengthens me.'"

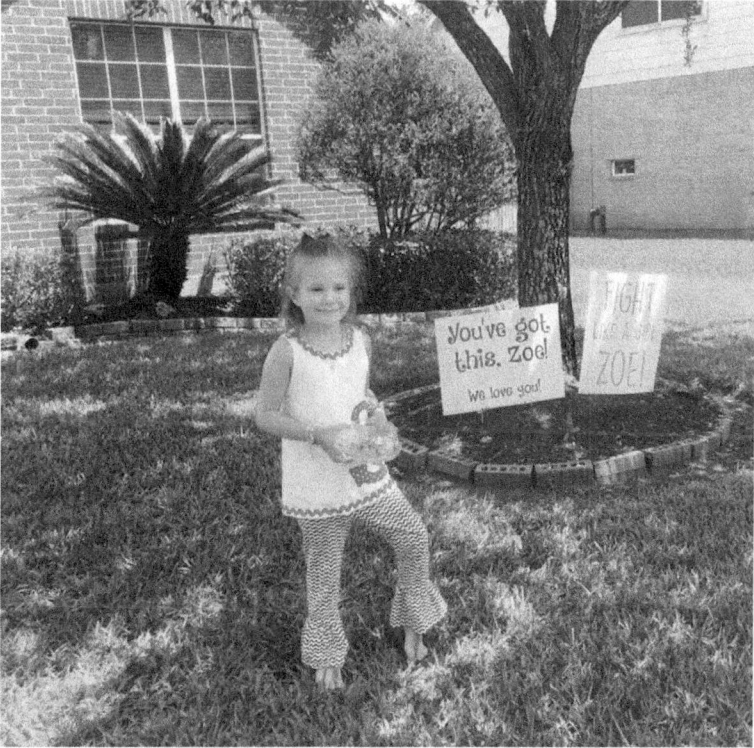

Meme Alice helped us sort through all the wonderful gifts, cards, and letters we'd received from our sweet friends.

We offer our deepest gratitude to those who have supported our family. Your prayers and encouragement have been a beautiful blessing to us. Her achievements have encouraged people who've never believed. God has used her sickness for His glory.

Zoe slept well in *her* bed that first night. We had installed a video monitor in her room so we could hear and see her if she needed us. Her dog Sophie that had visited her in the hospital a week before was delighted to see her.

As I write this, several weeks have passed since Zoe's release from the hospital. There's still work ahead of us, and she's willing to try. She's a fighter. We have enrolled her in *Open Door Therapy Center* here in Houston. Here she is with her therapists, Mrs. Michelle and Mrs. Amber.

Zoe has also begun taking piano lessons from my childhood friend, Mandy Meeks Rushing.

Sophie, Zoe's puppy, was extremely pleased to have her home.

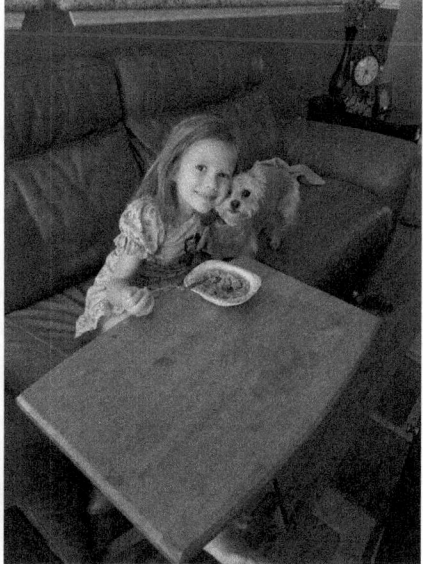

It wasn't long before the music returned.

Watch a brief video of Zoe back home at:
http://tinyurl.com/y92d5gek

On the Fourth of July, our subdivision honored Zoe in the park. She arrived in a CyFair Fire Department fire truck with her friends, who had prayed for her while she was hospitalized.

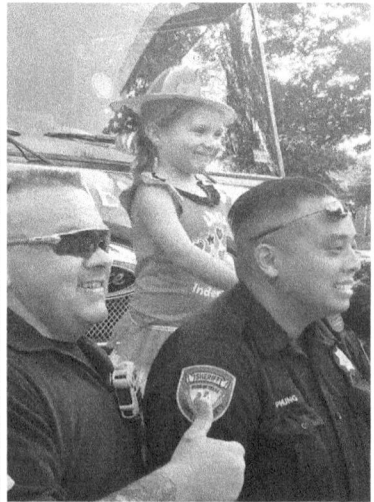

She was gracious and poised considering all the attention.

Watch two brief videos of Zoe's arrival at the park:

http://tinyurl.com/y7963o9l

http://tinyurl.com/y6uzymv3

After the honors, she spent the rest of the afternoon in the pool. Swimming is one of the few doctor-approved activities.

Zoe is a fun-loving, outgoing young lady who loves her friends.

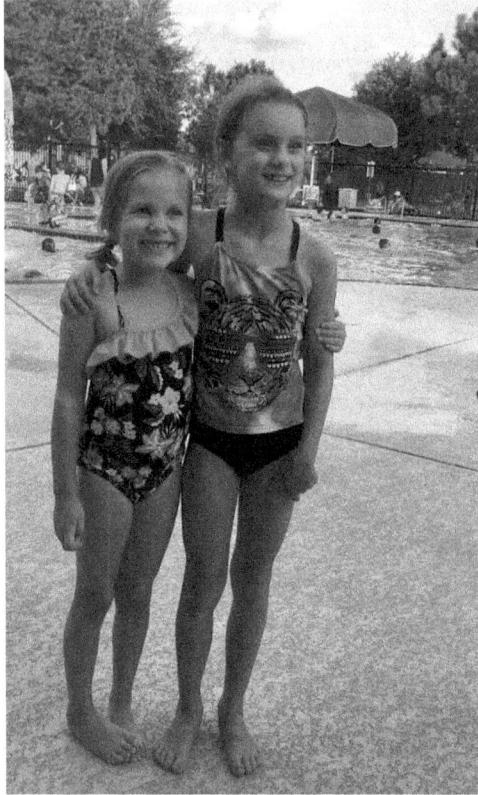

Olivia is Zoe's best friend. They are like sisters.

19

15 LESSONS LEARNED

One doesn't need to live to old age to learn that life can be challenging. It can throw you some curves. It's quite unpredictable. Bad things happen to good people and kids. But it's not what happens to us, as much as it is how we respond to what happens to us that shapes our lives.

I feel after sharing our story; it would be good to leave you with a list of some lessons we learned. (They are not necessarily in any particular order.)

We are not perfect people. We look at this miracle and wonder why God chose to share this with us. In this life, we won't find answers to all our questions, but we can sow into the lives of others as we recognize their needs. We'll take the opportunity to give back, pay it forward, and share the love that we've felt. As my granddaddy always said, "What we've received is on its way to someone else. Our job is to make sure it gets to them."

1. God loves you and is for you, no matter who you are, where you're from, or what you've done.

2. Expect times of uncertainty. They will come. We live on a fallen planet filled with broken people. There will be times of fear, regret, doubt, and uncertainty. But don't dwell on those things. Instead, remain focused on Him. Trust Him alone with all things. Pray expectantly, with thanksgiving. (Philippians 4:6-8)

3. Love your family. There are no perfect families. Each of us has baggage and burdens. Life can change in an instant. I learned how much my husband loves us, and how much I love him and our children

4. Be real. It's okay to believe God's plan for your life, but understand that life at its best isn't always cupcakes and rainbows. Be honest with those you trust, and with God. Having feelings is okay. We're human.

5. Take everything with a grain of salt. What may be the right answer for today, may not fit the issue of tomorrow. Don't get stuck in the moment or hang onto one piece of the pie. There's more to come.

6. Admit when you're wrong. Being wrong is okay. We are all wrong from time to time. We're not perfect. We are "under construction." When you are wrong, offer an apology when needed. It will rid you of regret later. Apologize and be free!

7. Learn from your mistakes. "To thine own self be true." (Wm Shakespeare) No one else can live your life for you. Mistakes happen. Don't deny them or run from them. Learn from your mistakes and grow!

8. Cherish time with those you love. We never know what tomorrow may bring. If someone you care for is taken from this world tomorrow, would you be confident that they knew how special they were to you?

9. Don't sweat the small stuff. "Be anxious for nothing…" (Philippians 4:6)

10. Stay positive. Negativity will drag you down. Look for the silver lining behind every cloud. Be strong, and believe. Encourage others, and they'll encourage you.

11. Establish an eternal living relationship with God and talk with Him as a friend, often. Allow His presence to bring you peace. When the doctors say, "There is no way." Boldly say, "But God!" God has the final word. Not the medical team, your family, or your friends.

12. Know that your true friends will stand beside you. They will share your burdens and see past your smile to your broken heart.

13. Children are priceless treasures that God entrusts to us. Handle them with care.

14. You are stronger than you know. Through this journey, I learned that I'm stronger than I realized. God has the final say. My husband and family love me unconditionally. Like all marriages, my hubby Chris and I have our ups and downs. But I can't imagine having to have faced this with anyone other than him.

15. Don't be afraid to ask for help. It's okay to lean on those you love and trust. We all feel defeated at times. God is strong in our weakness. Reach out to those around you and ask for their help.

The word "Zoe" is the Greek word for life!

Zoe is a little canvas on which God painted
His compassionate healing grace.

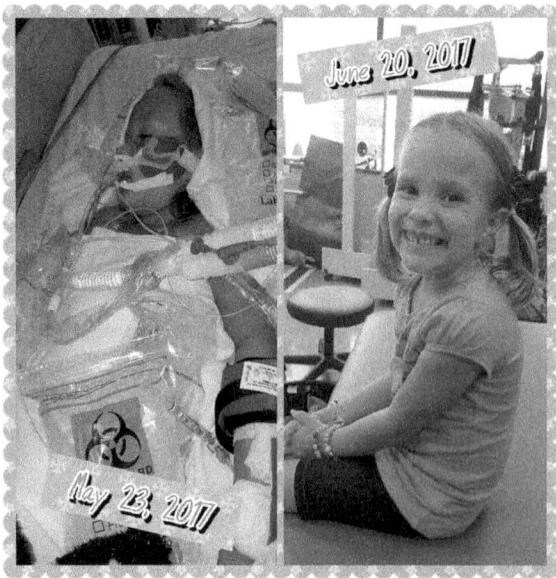

Watch Zoe sing Mandisa's song, "Overcomer"
Zoe is a real life Overcomer
http://tinyurl.com/y97texpr

NOTES:

1. http://bit.ly/Ashlees-Essential-Oil

www.ingramcontent.com/pod-product-compliance
Lightning Source LLC
LaVergne TN
LVHW051133080426
835510LV00018B/2391